Meeting-Space Ideas

Space Ideas

for Youth Ministry

by
Todd Outcalt

Group
Loveland, Colorado

dedication

To Chelsey and Logan,
future teenagers

Meeting-Space Ideas for Youth Ministry

Copyright © 1998 Todd Outcalt

CREDITS
Editor: Amy Simpson
Chief Creative Officer: Joani Schultz
Copy Editor: Julie Meiklejohn
Designer and Art Director: Jean Bruns
Cover Art Director: Jeff Storm
Cover Designer: Elise Lansdon
Computer Graphic Artist: Randy Kady
Cover Photographer: Jafe Parsons
Illustrator: Paula Becker
Production Manager: Gingar Kunkel

Library of Congress Cataloging-in-Publication Data
Outcalt, Todd.
    Meeting-space ideas for youth ministry / by Todd Outcalt.
       p. cm.
    Includes indexes.
    ISBN 0-7644-2026-7 (alk. paper)
    1. Church group work with youth--Equipment and supplies.
2. Church decoration and ornament. 3. Interior decoration.
I. Title.
BV4447.O78 1997
254'.7--dc21
                                                      97-39561
                                                         CIP

10 9 8 7 6 5 4 3 2 1   07 06 05 04 03 02 01 00 99 98

Printed in the United States of America.

Contents

Ideas

acknowledgments

Much thanks to the many churches and youth groups who opened their doors and shared their ideas with me, even when they didn't know it.

Thank you to Amy Simpson and the staff at Group Publishing who took a germ of an idea and turned it into a decent book.

And thanks to my family—especially Becky—who have sacrificed through the entire process and cheered me on.

Finally, with much appreciation and gratitude, I thank the hundreds of teenagers over the years who have allowed me to be their friend and pastor. You have made this book, and I cherish you all. Here's to the memories...

Montmorenci United Methodist Church
Fair Promise and High Falls United Methodist Churches
Methodist Temple (Terre Haute)
Youngstown
Noblesville First
Methodist Temple (Evansville)

Introduction

When I was a teenager, my youth group (all three of us) gathered in a back room of the church basement—a dark, dank space that smelled heavily of fuel oil and the stagnant limewater lingering in the sump pump pit. It wasn't pretty, but it was home.

Several years later, when I was in college, I began to visit other churches and found that not all youth centers were created equal. Few were fancy and expensive-looking, but most seemed to have an adequate sense of decor and spirit—the type of space that would be pleasing and inviting to teenagers.

In my years as a youth worker, as I've visited other churches, I've always made it a point to peek into their youth centers. I've made notes of features I wanted to incorporate into the teen center back home. Many of the ideas inspired me, some enlightened me, and a few provided the perfect ideas my youth group needed to create a new look in the youth center.

Good space can be difficult to find these days, even in the church. We have rooms, but we don't utilize them to their full potential. The church seems to be slow to acknowledge this reality.

Schools, on the other hand, are catching on. When I took my daughter to her first day of elementary school, I was stunned by the creative use of space—the colorful displays, the wall charts and posters, the learning centers, and the computer corners. It was obvious that the teachers had spent a great deal of time working on the rooms themselves, preparing them for the students.

As I thought about this preparation, I realized that many youth leaders, pastors, and church boards give minimal consideration to the significance of space and decor in the church. Or perhaps they give much attention to the sanctuary or worship center while neglecting the educational facilities for children and teenagers.

The ideas in this book don't focus exclusively on decor, though. You'll also find ideas concerning alternative meeting places; new ways to utilize existing features; a host of ways to involve your teenagers in creating a youth area that's attractive, warm, and inviting; and outlines for using your youth area as a resource in your ministry.

There truly is a theology attached to the space we use—not only in our worship areas, but everywhere in the church building. For this reason, it's important that youth leaders utilize their youth areas to their maximum potential. Our outreach and ministry to teenagers can make an enormous difference in their lives, especially if we can help teenagers feel welcome and "at home" by providing wonderful meeting places.

Visit a teenager's bedroom, and you'll instantly recognize how important space and decor can be. Every teenager wants his or her own space, and teenagers tend to decorate their rooms to express their individuality. We can encourage them to do the same with youth centers and meeting places.

By using some of the ideas in this book, your youth group might be able to transform even a dank and smelly church-basement room into a magnificent place of fellowship, worship, and learning.

Meeting-Space Ideas for Youth Ministry is actually a simple book. This volume is a collection of creative ideas designed to help your youth group use its space in the church building or another meeting place to its greatest advantage. The book also provides youth workers with information about cost, materials needed for each project, an overview of the amount of time and work involved in making each idea effective, bonus ideas, and valuable suggestions that will help make each project fun and exciting.

You'll find wonderful opportunities for fellowship, discussion, and learning. Each project idea includes an active-learning lesson, a game, an object lesson, a discussion starter, or a service project that can help your teenagers encounter God or draw closer to each other.

You'll also find suggestions for overcoming obstacles and tips for adapting these ideas to a variety of spaces. The end of this book features helpful indexes that will enable you to find ideas and themes quickly.

Should you find yourself in a church that doesn't have a space designated for teenagers, don't worry. This book can help you create your own youth space by using some ideas from other churches working under similar circumstances.

Many of the ideas in this book are being happily used by dozens, if not hundreds, of churches. Most youth leaders are actively engaged in trying to make their youth spaces more inviting and effective. They welcome new ideas, many of which will prompt them, with the help of church leaders and teenagers, to design spaces that are unique to their particular ministries, gifts, and needs.

Many of the ideas in this book can be used on a rotating basis. A youth room doesn't have to look the same for decades. It can look different every month. And since most of the ideas aren't permanent, creative youth workers can use the ideas to add new variety every year.

Whether you want to give your present youth room a much-needed face lift, you're looking for some unique decorating ideas, you simply want to change the appearance of your room from time to time, or you're dying for some new themes and activities for youth meetings, this book will help you give your teenagers the kind of meeting place and meeting time that will keep them coming back.

As you use this book, no doubt you'll discover that your meeting place can be a great resource in your youth ministry. If teenagers enjoy gathering in the space your group has created together, they'll be more willing to invite others, they'll learn and share more openly, and they'll know that they're part of something special.

And who knows? You might discover that your youth room is one of your greatest assets!

Why IS Space Important?

So why is youth meeting-space so important? Isn't it enough that you have enticing programs, dynamic people, and effective planning? Youth ministry, after all, is about people, not spaces and materials. And in some churches, good meeting space is harder to come by than good seats at the Super Bowl. Why be picky?

What we do with the space we have can be a grand act of stewardship. Because God has provided a place to minister to young people, why not make that space the most inviting, comfortable haven it can be? Meeting space can also become a reflection of our intentions in ministry. And in the meantime, a meeting space can become a valuable ministry resource in teaching students about God's love.

Architecture has always been important to people of faith. The ways in which space is utilized for worship, learning, and fellowship profoundly affect and reflect our understanding of God and others.

The ancient Israelites, for example, devoted much time, energy, and effort to the construction of both the portable desert tabernacle (Exodus 36) and later the temple in Jerusalem (1 Kings 6-9). We know the ancient tabernacle was used for a variety of purposes and was decorated with an abundance of beautiful objects (Exodus 37-40) such as golden lampstands, an ark containing the Mosaic law on stone, an altar to receive the sacrifices of God's people, ornate priestly garments, and luxurious curtains.

Long after the temple was built, the author of Revelation

wrote of a vision of the heavenly Jerusalem with golden streets, pearl gates, and walls inlaid with precious stones (Revelation 21:10-27).

Throughout the Middle Ages, great cathedrals and basilicas were erected in Europe—grand churches with spires straining toward the heavens, vast spaces of beauty to remind people of the awesome power and mystery of God.

Judeo-Christian history is characterized by the notion that our theology is displayed in the shape of our architecture and the space we employ for worshiping and learning about God. The Christian faith has attempted to inspire people to live greater lives, dream larger dreams, look toward a heavenly home, and serve God and neighbor. One of the ways we all aspire to fulfill God's will for our lives and our world is by sharing space together.

Space, after all, is sacred. God has created the space in which we live—namely, the earth. God entrusted us to order it, give it name and meaning, and fill it with purpose.

The space we designate for young people should never be boring or drab. Youth rooms can become sacred spaces when we help teenagers use their own creativity, culture, personalities, and music to form holy places. In fact, a great youth room might not appeal to adults at all! But teenagers will instantly recognize and experience God's presence whenever they enter a space they have helped to create and beautify for that purpose.

That's what this book is about.

what's in a youth room?

Take a walk around your church facilities—especially your teen center, youth room, or other space designated for youth gatherings and meetings. As you consider the space in your church facility and think about the needs of the teenagers in your church and community, you'll naturally want this room to take on a special significance and role. The way this room is decorated and arranged does make a difference!

Consider, for example, the colors in your youth center.

Are they inviting and cheerful or drab and depressing? Do the furnishings make teenagers want to gather in the room for fellowship and learning or turn and run? Is the space arranged so it's conducive to laughter and friendship, or is it boring? These questions should be important to youth leaders, pastors, and church leadership.

A great youth room doesn't have to be an expensive, high-tech masterpiece. While on a rafting trip in West Virginia, our youth group spent the night at a small church in the mountains. It was a quaint church building with no designated space for teenagers. There were only a few rooms, including a fellowship area and one bathroom. My teenagers seemed perplexed by this tiny building. "They must not have any teenagers in this church," one of my adult chaperones remarked.

But before we left the next day, we discovered that the church did indeed have a vital youth ministry.

"Our youth group meets in the restaurant across the street," one of the church members told us. "Our youth leader runs the place, and the kids meet in a back room every Sunday morning for breakfast and study. They meet there again on Sunday nights for more fun and learning."

I journeyed across the street and found a wonderful back room in that restaurant which the owner had devoted to teenagers. It was a marvelous setup, with pinball machines, posters, music, and a rack of study Bibles. I could tell that the teenagers had a great deal of pride in their meeting place.

Before I left the restaurant, the owner gave me an important reminder: "You know," he said, "we've found that teenagers love to make their own space. Having a place they can call home is important to them. And it doesn't have to be in a church. We've had some wonderful discussions in this back room—and a lot of fun. The place just keeps getting better and better."

I like that perspective. It has helped me remember that space is important—especially for the people of God.

creating an awesome place

You don't have to spend wads of money to create a teen

room suitable to the task of youth ministry. All it takes is a little ingenuity, determination, and some helping hands to make space come alive.

As you begin to think about the use of space in your church, consider the story of Jacob in Genesis 28:10-22. After stealing his brother's blessing, Jacob was forced to flee from Esau. He left his parents and journeyed toward the far country of his ancestors—forsaken, alone, and afraid. One night Jacob fell asleep and dreamed of a ladder reaching into the heavens. In his dream he saw angels of God descending and ascending the ladder. And God gave him the blessing of Abraham.

When Jacob awoke, he said, "Surely the Lord is in this place, but I did not know it!" As a memorial, Jacob took a stone, set it up as a pillar, and poured oil over it. He called that place "Bethel," which means "the house of God."

This story can illustrate the importance of space—not only for worship but also for learning. The story of Jacob is a reminder that God may be encountered in particular places at particular times.

Every youth room can be a place where teenagers encounter God. How does your youth room help bring teenagers together? Is it warm and inviting? Does the room provide visual reminders of community and love? Are there signs of God's presence? What are some ways you can help teenagers recognize God's presence as they enter your youth area?

These were the types of questions I was asking years ago when I helped start an after-school program for teenagers and middle school children at our church. Our space was a large, open room with little color and vibrancy. Our only advantage was that this space was located near the middle school and the bus stop. We were accessible, but we knew we had to do something with the room to help convey a feeling of excitement, joy, and love.

First we asked an artist in our congregation to make a beautiful, multicolored banner featuring the name of our new program. We positioned a snack table immediately inside the door. We set up study areas, draped a parachute across the ceiling, and placed posters on the walls. We set up a tripod with a video camera and played lively music.

The first day was a real test of nerves for me and all the other volunteers. Many of the children and teenagers came from troubled homes and were at-risk students. A high percentage had never been inside a church building. A few were hyperactive, some could not stop talking, and others acted out aggressively. At one point a fight broke out.

We tried to be friendly, upbeat, and patient. We dispensed smiles and helped with homework. We made a valiant attempt to create a warm and inviting space that was exciting and unique. We tried to teach the children about God. And we wondered what we had gotten ourselves into.

Near the end of our time together that first day, something happened that made us realize that our efforts had made a difference. As the kids were leaving, one young man lingered by the doorway, munching on a cookie. He looked around the room a final time, inspected the parachute hanging from the ceiling, winked at the silent video camera, and smiled through his braces. Then he said: "Wow! This place is awesome! See you next week!" And with that, he bolted out the door.

As you read through the ideas in this book, I hope you'll welcome the opportunity to make your youth room an awesome place. I hope you'll engage your youth group in the process of making its own meaningful space. The activities, learning opportunities, and games in this book will help the members of your group take each idea and make it their own.

After you've completed a few of these projects, I hope your teenagers will be able to say, "God is in this place, and it's awesome!"

Overcoming Obstacles

O K, so you like the idea of renovating the youth meeting-space. But now you're probably asking: "How much will it cost? What if the church board doesn't approve? What if there is no space? What happens to all our old furnishings if they are replaced?"

And if you're not asking these questions now, chances are someone on the church board will.

Fortunately, there are many options for creating a top-notch youth center. And most of them don't have to cost a great deal of money or cause a load of misery.

finding money

The ideas in this book include average costs for most of the items. The bulk of these items cost little or nothing—and many others you can probably obtain through donations. Your own creativity and regular group resources should be adequate to carry out most of the decorating ideas in this book.

However, in the event that you're planning some major renovations or you hope to persuade the church board to sign that hefty bank note, let me first offer a few suggestions about money and financing in the church. Anyone who is in ministry has, from time to time, run up against that brick wall commonly known as "budget." But in the event that you find yourself constantly working with an anemic bank account, don't despair. Remember, many of the ideas in this book cost very little.

Should you have budget constraints, turn to the cost index in the back of this book, find the ideas that fit your budget range, and go from there. Or try using your own creativity to adapt ideas to fit your budget.

Should you want to try an idea or two that cost a bit more, you might find that you can achieve your goal over time. Save a little here and there when you can. Have an extra fund-raiser or two. Or give the church a few extra months or years to come up with the funding.

Also, don't forget that you can seek donations from a variety of sources. I've found that many individuals in the church are happy to contribute to specific projects, especially ones for children and teenagers. You might also receive donations from businesses, service organizations, and men's and women's clubs.

dealing with church folks

Another problem youth leaders may encounter is running up against resistant church members. Every now and then, a youth worker will experience resistance from someone in the church who doesn't like change.

In the event that you'll be dealing with resistant church members, you might begin by preparing your own answers to a few basic questions:

- What changes are you proposing to make, and why?
- Who will be served by these changes, and how?
- How often will you use the room? weekly? daily?
- What dreams do you have for making use of this space?
- How do these changes relate to your philosophy of youth ministry?

After you've answered these questions in your own mind, be prepared to share your answers with church leaders and other influential souls who will be making decisions or discussing your proposals. Help them understand that there is a philosophy behind your requests. Stress the point that your ideas are for the benefit of the teenagers.

Once you've expressed your dream and demonstrated how you'll use your resources, give the church people ample time to prepare for your request and to achieve the goal. For example, it stands to reason that a church will be more willing to fund a room project at $500 per year for three years as opposed to $1500 in a single year. Plan ahead, and try not to ask for more than you need.

By helping church members see the importance of youth ministry in your church, you should be able to gain the support and funding you will need. Try to present a balanced picture of all that the youth ministry program has accomplished, what it's about, and what you hope to achieve. Help the church leaders see the big picture by sharing your vision and your dreams.

Best of all, tell your stories. Relate a few real-life situations in your youth ministry. Help church members see that they're part of something real and vital and that their decisions can make the difference in the lives of teenagers. Who knows? You might even receive some unexpected help from people in your church!

inadequate spaces

Another hurdle for many congregations is finding an adequate space for youth ministry. All the wonderful ideas in the world don't go very far if one has only a five-by-five-foot closet to work with.

But there may be other options. Alternative spaces outside the church facility itself may be readily available or handily supplied. And some may be just right for your particular group size or makeup.

In this book you'll find several ideas for alternative meeting places. One or two of these might prove to be perfect for your group.

If you don't have a youth room, do a bit of networking within your church. Find out what alternative locations are available within your community. You might find a back room in a restaurant, a business office, a funeral home, or a summer cottage. You can still make a wonderful space for teenagers in one of these places.

old church buildings

I often meet youth leaders who are dejected because the church buildings they meet in are growing old and dilapidated. The buildings themselves aren't attractive to younger people—especially teenagers. And if these churches have youth rooms, they're often stuffy and inadequate.

I would like to be able to say that I have all the answers to such problems, but I don't. But I have seen some top-notch youth rooms in ancient church buildings—inner-city structures that from the outside didn't appear attractive at all.

For example, one inner-city church I visited had expended enormous resources and effort to attract teenagers who normally roamed the streets. This church had made several professional-looking signs that advertised its Friday-night youth center—an open basketball court with pinball machines, a jukebox, and plenty of adult helpers. Their youth center worked, seemingly because the entire church had rallied behind the ministry and saw it as a vital resource it had to offer.

I've seen other youth rooms in older churches which, though small, were bright and attractive. The rooms had been thoroughly cleaned and deodorized. Attention was given to music, posters, and a fun atmosphere—powerful components of any youth ministry. In spite of the fact that these church buildings were old, the youth areas were inviting and warm. Many of these churches also gave special attention to advertising—working with the school newspapers—or hosting special events.

If your youth room is located in an old building, I suggest that you begin with a basic make over—paint, furnishings, and music. Make what you have as attractive to teenagers as you possibly can. Then try to expand your ministry by doing creative advertising and holding exciting events.

Or you might consider meeting at an alternative site. Do some brainstorming to see if you might be able to locate a room somewhere in your neighborhood. There's no law that says you must meet in a church building to have an effective youth ministry.

If you choose to meet somewhere else, though, make sure your group will be covered by insurance if anything goes wrong.

ugly furnishings

Perhaps you're asking, "If I buy new furnishings for the youth room, how do I dispose of the two green lounge chairs and the donated flowered sofa?" Obviously some transitions are more sensitive than others. Old and ugly furnishings, particularly if they've been donated by church members, may prove to be a delicate issue.

There are options, though. You might choose to donate the old furnishings to a thrift store, a shelter, or some other worthwhile ministry. In this way, the old furnishings can still be of use to someone else. You might "retire" the old furnishings or give them away.

If these options don't work for you and you're still stuck with ugly furnishings, you might try to find some coverings for chairs and sofas. They're available in most retail stores for a reasonable price, or perhaps a seamstress in your church could sew them. Still another option is to advertise the need for new furnishings in your church bulletin. I did this once and ended up with nearly a dozen assorted chairs and sofas from which to choose. I kept the best pieces, explained the situation on thank-you notes to everyone who made donations, and sold the furnishings I didn't need (putting the money into the youth fund). Everyone seemed pleased to contribute in one way or another.

On the other hand, if you're looking to have the latest furnishings or the most stylish pieces, you might want to come up with a long-term plan. Buy one or two pieces of furniture each year until you have what you need.

multipurpose rooms

Not every church has a designated space for teenagers. Some churches are forced to make use of multipurpose rooms. If this is true of your church, you know that the youth group is only one of many groups that utilize the space.

This reality can pose a problem for those who might want to adapt a multipurpose room for teenagers. Perhaps there isn't enough space, the room is too cluttered, or some church members are opposed to making sweeping changes in appearance or decor.

If you're challenged by such a situation, you might consider some of the following options.

Perhaps you could gain permission to dedicate one corner of the room to youth ministry. The use of wall space could be used to your advantage, and the teenagers could gain some ownership for a section of the room.

You might work with the church board to remodel the entire room. Again, share your vision of the project and talk about how other groups might benefit from the changes. For example, many of the projects in this book could be used for groups of all ages. Other people who use the room might be willing to share in the effort and expense.

Or you might look at the ideas in this book that are portable. Perhaps you could store your youth ministry items in a closet and then move them into the multipurpose room when you need them. With a little planning, you could make even a temporary spot seem like home.

As you begin to plan your next project, keep in mind that youth ministry is not centrally about physical structures or decor. Youth ministry is about people—teenagers and their families. All the ideas in this book are merely means to an end: namely, that teenagers will grow in their own discipleship and faith.

A room can never take the place of good fellowship, inspiring worship, or thought-provoking lessons. But a room can be an instrument of God's grace and a means of drawing closer to others.

Walls & More

CHRISTIAN-MUSIC POSTERS

COST: *$0*
WORK LEVEL: *easy*
TIME INVOLVED: *instant*
MATERIALS: *Christian-music posters and tape or tacks*

If the walls of your youth room need a face lift but you don't have much of a budget, think about hanging some posters. Each month, most Christian bookstores receive a new inventory of display posters for Christian music. Over the years, I've picked up dozens of these free posters simply by asking store managers for extras or by asking managers to call me when the old ones are taken down. The next time you make a visit to a Christian bookstore, ask the manager if you might have a few extra posters. If there are no extras available, ask if you might leave your name and number. Most managers will be glad to give you a call when old posters are taken down.

Don't forget the secular music stores that carry a wide selection of music styles. They too receive Christian-music posters. Chances are, they throw these posters away. A few freebies could be yours for the asking.

Once you have your posters, you may want to laminate them and glue them to cardboard for a better-quality appearance. Hang the posters throughout the youth room, and add new posters from time to time.

If music is important in your ministry, you might also try featuring an "artist of the month." Use a poster to highlight that musician.

bonus idea

In addition to the Christian-music posters, mix in a few posters of movie stars, professional athletes, and other famous individuals. Encourage teenagers to discuss the impact of secular culture on their lives and how Christians should respond to secular society.

For some artists, you can pick up posters as well as displays that highlight information about the artists.

Once a poster has been on the wall for a while, be sure to take it down and put up a new one in its place. Give the old poster away, award it as a prize, or auction it off at a fund-raiser.

devotion

Fame and Fortune

THEMES: *faithfulness, fame and fortune, music*
MATERIALS: *chalk and a chalkboard or markers and newsprint, Bibles, index cards, pencils, Christian-music posters, and tape or tacks*

This devotion will help your teenagers think about the allure of fame and fortune—even in Christian ministry. Before this devotion, write the following Scripture references on a chalkboard or a piece of newsprint:

- I John 2:12-14
- I John 2:15-17
- I John 3:2-3
- I John 3:18-22
- I John 5:1-5

To begin the devotion, display the Christian-music posters and then read the following letter aloud:

> *Congratulations!*
>
> *You've just been named the contemporary Christian-music artist of the year. You've signed a three-record deal with a record label, and you'll be appearing on national television. Thousands of people will be buying your albums. Your name will be known in churches across the country, you'll make a lot of money, and people will want your autograph. You'll be on the road most of the time, touring the country. Life is great—you're on the road to stardom!*

After reading the letter to the group, give each person an index card and a pencil. Say: **Now that you're famous, I'd like you to write down a few facts about yourself. Tell me how you'll handle this fame and fortune. Be specific about how you'll use your time, your talent, and your money.**

Give the group several minutes to complete the assignment and then ask:

- How does it feel to be famous?

bonus idea

Instead of asking students what their publicity posters would look like if they were Christian-music artists, provide art supplies and invite kids to make posters.

● How is your life different from the way it used to be?

● What are some new temptations you face now that you're famous and wealthy?

Turn students' attention to the Scripture references you've written on the chalkboard or newsprint. Have teenagers form five groups, and assign each group a Bible passage. (It's OK for a "group" to consist of one person.) Instruct teenagers to look up the passages and to discuss the following questions in their groups (you may want to write the questions on newsprint and display them where everyone can refer to them):

● What does this Scripture passage say about living the Christian life?

● What does this passage say about fame and fortune?

● What can this Scripture passage teach us about the desire to obtain material things?

When groups have finished their discussions, invite a few students to summarize their Scripture passages in their own words and tell what their groups discussed. Ask:

● If you were to make a music poster for yourself, what would it look like?

● Based on the Scripture passages we've read, what do you think your responsibility would be as a Christian artist?

● How would this responsibility be reflected on your poster?

Close the devotion by having students discuss this question:

● If you became famous and wealthy, how do you think your new lifestyle would affect your faith? How would your faith affect your new lifestyle?

EVENT CALENDAR

COST: *$0-$25*
WORK LEVEL: *easy*
TIME INVOLVED: *instant*
MATERIALS: *one of the following items: a large wall calendar, a dry-erase board, a chalkboard, poster board, cardboard, a bulletin board, or a blank wall; and tape or tacks*

Posting an event calendar on the wall can be a helpful way to communicate with your group. Even though you probably send out newsletters and postcards, not everyone gets your message the first time or even the second. Most youth leaders will admit that teenagers need constant reminders of upcoming events and projects, especially as their schedules fill up with school activities and other commitments. Many kids procrastinate until the last minute about making a commitment to attend an event, and some don't seem to know what's going on in the youth group even if they attend youth meetings regularly.

If you have teenagers like this in your youth group, a wall calendar can function as a constant reminder and communication tool. You can take advantage of a large format to highlight important events, call attention to dates and times, and assist teenagers who help with the scheduling of events.

Over the years I've seen some marvelous event calendars in youth rooms: posters scattered with cartoons, dry-erase boards highlighted with colorful illustrations, and display racks that open to reveal yearlong lists of upcoming events. One youth room featured a mascot (a life-size stuffed gorilla) holding a sign with information about the next service project. Another room used the inside of a door as the calendar—it was a slimy green color, and it sported the words "Don't read this! For adults only!" (This was a sure-fire way to get the teenagers to read it.)

As for the calendar itself, poster board will do; so will cardboard, a dry-erase board, a chalkboard, a blank painted wall, or almost any other large, flat surface. Use your imagination!

A wall calendar doesn't have to be boring. Take advantage of the space—add funny cartoons, quotes from members of your youth group, or photos. Some groups save their old wall calendars as keepsakes. Others have erasable wall calendars. Any format will do, as long as it conveys the information essential to your ministry.

object lesson

Days of Our Lives

THEMES: *God's sovereignty, priorities, stress, time*
MATERIALS: *a wall calendar, Bibles, and tape or tacks*

A wall calendar can serve as a unique object lesson for teenagers. Like most adults, many of today's kids live by their calendars. Many teenagers now carry pagers, electronic calendars, and pocket calendars at school. They know about crammed schedules, fast-paced lifestyles, and pressure.

Build on this real-life connection by using this idea to kick off a new year.

When you put up your new wall calendar, have teenagers form a circle around the calendar and ask:

● Why has saving time become such a priority for people in our society?

● How does the desire to save time affect the way you live your life?

Read aloud Ecclesiastes 3:1-13. Invite a few students to paraphrase the passage in their own words.

Say: **The writer of Ecclesiastes was wise and wanted to help people understand that we can only control so much of what goes on around us. Ultimately, we're at the mercy of circumstances, God's created order, and the purposes of God. It's our responsibility to discern "what time it is" and act accordingly. When we look at a calendar, we can be reminded that God is in control and that everything that happens is part of God's plan. We can look at our circumstances and determine what we can do to bring glory to God at that time.**

bonus idea

Continue this experience by holding a brainstorming session to begin planning upcoming events. Help the teenagers stay focused on making the most of their time while also accepting God's grace and freedom to find times of laughter, joy, relaxation, and happiness. Encourage them to plan activities that fill all the "times" they listed in their rewriting of Ecclesiastes 3:1-8.

Ask:

● As we look at our empty wall-calendar today, what are some activities we can do to bring glory to God?

● How can we evaluate our circumstances to determine what we should focus on at any particular time?

• What role does planning ahead play in relying on God's sovereignty?

Encourage kids to rewrite Ecclesiastes 3:1-8, listing as many "times" as they can think of that will apply specifically to their lives. For example, kids might write "There is a time to go to school and a time to stay home. There is a time to wake up early and a time to sleep in."

ORIGINAL ART

COST: *$0-$50*
WORK LEVEL: *moderate*
TIME INVOLVED: *short-term*
MATERIALS: *art supplies (such as paint, clay, canvas, and brushes) or a completed original work of art and tape or tacks*

Perhaps I've been lucky, but in every congregation I've served there has been at least one accomplished artist. And in my opinion, people who work in the arts are some of the most underutilized people in the church. We rarely consider their gifts when thinking about worship, education, and outreach. In many churches, we tend to admire what they do but ask nothing of their talents.

When I began asking artists to create original works for a youth room, I was amazed at the results. I ended up with some of the best artwork I could have imagined—colorful, exciting canvases and sculptures. And the teenagers loved them.

Usually, when we begin looking for artwork, we head straight for prints of famous paintings and buy framed works by long-dead artists. But that isn't your only option. A good artist in your congregation would probably be willing to offer his or her talent to your teenagers free of charge (although you might have to provide the materials). And with a few suggestions from your teenagers, the artist would probably be able to produce an original work for your youth room that everyone can be excited about. Ask around—you might be surprised to find a top-notch artist in your congregation.

worship idea

Re-Creation

THEMES: *the Bible, creation*

MATERIALS: *canvases, water-based paints, paintbrushes, smocks, tape or tacks, and a Bible*

So what if you can't find an artist in your congregation? Your youth group can create its own original art! Head down to your local art store and buy a few canvases (the ones already stretched on frames work best), some water-based paints, paintbrushes, and smocks. Bring them back to the youth room and try this one-of-a-kind worship experience. You'll have a great time of worship, and you'll end up with original art that you can hang in the youth room.

bonus idea

If you think your original works of art are something special, why not use them as a fundraiser? Sell the youth group's paintings and use the money for a mission project.

You'll probably want to choose a day when you can take the youth group outside. This is not an indoor activity unless you cover your entire floor with newspapers or plastic. Spread the canvases on the ground, prepare the paints and brushes, and then read aloud Psalm 19:1-6. Say: **Let's give thanks to God for the beauty of creation. We're going to worship God by producing artwork that will remind us of the power, wonder, and majesty of God's universe.**

Set out the paints, and give a paintbrush and a smock to each person. Say: **I'm going to read aloud the story of God's creation of the universe. As I read each verse, I'd like you to** place one color—only one—on the canvas in any fashion you choose. Use your imagination. After you've completed your dab, swipe, or stroke of the brush, I'll read the next verse. Respond worshipfully to each verse and then our work will be complete.

Invite teenagers to dab, swipe, stroke, or slosh the paint on the canvases as you read Genesis 1 slowly, one verse at a time. You might assign groups of teenagers to particular canvases, or you may want to allow everyone in the group to roam from canvas to canvas adding personal touches.

After you've read the Scripture and the painting is finished, close your worship experience with a moment of silence to ponder God's creative power, to look at the sky, and to admire the beauty of the outdoors. Then give each teenager an opportunity to express to God what he or she most appreciates about God's creation.

Clean up your supplies and then allow the canvases to dry completely before mounting them on the wall.

STUDENT OF THE MONTH

COST: *$0-$30*
WORK LEVEL: *easy*
TIME INVOLVED: *short-term*
MATERIALS: *empty wall space, photographs of teenagers in the youth group, and tape or tacks*

One of the most unique wall displays I've seen—a fantastic idea for building the morale of a youth group—was an idea called "Student of the Month." This wall display featured a picture of a teenager; a profile including information about his or her family, friends, hobbies, and interests; and a few pertinent quotes.

When I talked to the youth leader about this idea, he told me that at the end of each month he conducts a telephone interview with one of the teenagers. He asks questions about family and friends, sports, hobbies, and other interests. Then he writes up a profile and attaches it to a recent photograph.

He told me: "This way, we all get to know each other a little better and everyone feels important. I keep track of who I've interviewed and make certain that I include everyone, not just the most popular kids in school or the ones who have the highest grade point averages or the ones who play sports."

If you're planning to make photography an important part of your youth ministry, obviously you'll benefit from having a camera on hand. A good 35-mm camera sells for around $200. Taking a camera with you to every youth group event will keep you from saying, "What a great photo opportunity...if only I had a camera!"

group builder

News Release

THEMES: *excitement, fellowship, sharing faith*
MATERIALS: *telephones and an instant-print camera*

If you'd like to expand the idea of having a student of the month, try this telephone group-builder to get your group energized. This phone game will also help get your group excited for a new year.

Put together a list of all the teenagers in your youth group and their phone numbers, and arrange to have at least one instant-print camera on hand. Use the suggestions on page 30 to write an announcement about your upcoming meeting.

Arrange to have a few of your teenagers call the others in the group the day before the meeting. Give these teenagers the list of names and phone numbers of people in the group and a copy of the announcement you've written. Instruct them to call everyone else in the group and read the announcement over the phone. Then have them take pictures when other teenagers arrive at the meeting.

You may want to prepare your announcement in one of these two styles:

> Good evening. Our feature story tonight is about (name of youth group). At this hour it is reported that (names of a few young people) will be in attendance at an upcoming, highly controversial gathering. There will be plenty of (names of specific refreshments) for everyone! Astounding feats will be performed by (names of a few more young people). And (names of the teenager or teenagers assigned to take photographs) will greet people at the door and take their pictures. Inside sources tell us no one will want to miss this exciting event!
>
> Good evening, (name of student). Your mission, should you choose to accept it, is to attend this week's meeting of (name of youth group). Our sources tell us that (names of a few young people) will be in attendance. You will also see (names of a few more young people). Please be aware of hidden cameras as you enter the youth room. Someone will attempt to take your picture. This telephone message will self-destruct in one second.

WALL OF GUESTS

COST: *$0-$30*
WORK LEVEL: *easy*
TIME INVOLVED: *short-term*
MATERIALS: *empty wall space, an instant-print camera, instant-print film, and tape or tacks*

If you want to expand your photo opportunities while welcoming new young people into the group, try creating a "wall of guests." (You could also refer to it as a "wall of welcome," a "wall of newcomers," or a "wall of visitors.")

I used this idea for a year, simply using an instant-print camera to take snapshots of any guests and then posting the pictures on the wall along with names, addresses, phone numbers, and a few brief facts. This helped the students welcome new people and associate names with faces. It also helped me to track visitors and follow up with them.

Having a wall of guests can also encourage teenagers to keep coming back. Like adults, young people long to truly belong to a group. Helping them feel welcome and special from the beginning can go a long way.

Be sure to remove a photograph of a "guest" after a few weeks of attendance. As soon as a teenager feels at home with the group, consider him or her an intricate part of your fellowship.

devotion

Who's Missing?

THEMES: *acceptance, love, outreach, prayer*
MATERIALS: *a Bible, a free-standing candle or a candle in a candleholder, matches, and a chalkboard and chalk or newsprint and markers*

You can use your wall of guests in this closing devotion on love and acceptance. Have the group form a semicircle around the wall of guests. Put a lit candle in front of the students, and encourage them to spend a few moments in silence, studying the pictures on the wall and remembering those who have recently visited youth meetings. If you have visitors present at this meeting, introduce them to the rest of the group. Encourage them to participate in this devotion; this may be a great opportunity for them to see the love of God in action.

Say: **Sometimes it's difficult to get to know other people or to become friends with someone new. But the Bible tells us we can always be united with others in love. God's love draws us together, no matter who we are. If we reach out to others with the love of God, people will respond. This kind of outreach is very important, especially when someone is new to a group.**

Read 1 John 4:7-12 aloud. Then blow out the candle, and set an empty chair in front of the students.

Say: **This passage reminds us that our love begins with God's love for us. Love reaches out as God reaches out to each of us. Let's demonstrate love by reaching out to those who've been visiting our youth group. Look at the empty chair. Think about the people who have filled the empty chairs**

bonus idea

Allow a few of your teenagers to take responsibility for the wall of guests each week. Give them a camera, train them to take down pertinent information about visitors, and then step out of the way. You'll gain some new leaders in your group, and the teenagers will find that they have a ministry that is important to others.

31

in our group over the past several weeks. And consider who might fill that chair next week. Think about how you might show God's love this week to someone you don't know. Maybe you can make a phone call to someone who has visited our group recently. Maybe you could give a word of encouragement or a warm and sincere welcome to a visitor this week. Maybe you could give someone a ride to youth group.

Invite everyone to choose a partner. Say: **Tell your partner how you'll reach out this week to someone you don't know.** Give kids a few moments to talk and then say: **Now talk with your partner about ways our group can be more welcoming and loving to visitors. Talk about how we can show God's love to people we don't know.**

Close by asking each group to share its responses and writing these ideas on a chalkboard or newsprint. Keep the ideas posted for at least one month as a reminder to your group.

WALL OF PRAYER

COST: *$0-$10*
WORK LEVEL: *easy*
TIME INVOLVED: *instant*
MATERIALS: *empty wall space or a bulletin board, tacks or tape, and index cards*

The most famous wall of prayer is the western wall of the temple mount in Jerusalem. Both Jews and Gentiles go there from all over the world to offer prayers for the peace of Jerusalem, prayers for the healing of nations, and personal petitions to God. Some people bring their prayers on sheets of paper and stuff them into the cracks in the wall.

A meaningful "wall of prayer" in your youth room doesn't have to be so elaborate. All you need is a space devoted to prayer requests. A bulletin board will do nicely.

Each week, invite teenagers to write out prayer requests on index cards and post them on

bonus idea

You may want to encourage teenagers to post the answers to their prayers on the wall near the requests.

the wall or bulletin board. The requests can be anonymous or signed. Take a moment each week to pray for these requests.

ideas: walls & more

devotion

Symbols of Unity

THEMES: *cooperation, love, unity*
MATERIALS: *modeling clay (one color) and Bibles*

Use your wall of prayer to highlight the theme of unity.

Begin the devotion by giving a piece of modeling clay to each teenager. Then say: **I'd like everyone to work together to fashion a clay animal. There are only three rules: Everyone must participate, all the clay must be used, and you must complete the project in two minutes! Go!**

Look at your watch, and call time after two minutes. Ask the group:

● **What do you think of the animal you've created?**
● **Was this activity easy or difficult for you? Why?**

Give each person a Bible. Invite everyone to turn to 1 Corinthians 12:12-26. Read the passage aloud, or invite the teenagers to read aloud together from the same translation. Ask:

● **What does this passage tell us about unity?**
● **What does it say about working together?**

Say: **God wants us to have unity as Christian people. We may not always agree on everything and we may have conflicts, but we can still love one another and work together as disciples of Jesus. That's what unity means.**

Next, have a volunteer read aloud Ephesians 4:3-6. Ask:

● What are some obstacles to our unity?
● Why is unity sometimes difficult to achieve?
● Where does Christian unity begin?

bonus idea

As an extra demonstration of Christian unity, invite a youth group from another church or another denomination to join you for a prayer meeting.

Then say: God wants us to be unified. We can see this unity when we pray together, when we sing together, when we serve together, and when we have fun together. The Holy Spirit is our seal—our promise that God will preserve this unity. Our wall of prayer reminds us that we can maintain our unity by praying for each other. Prayer unites us in love and support, even when we aren't in the same room together.

Have teenagers form a circle and join hands. Say: As a sign of our unity, let's pray for the requests on our wall of prayer. We'll take turns praying aloud. If you don't want to pray aloud, squeeze the hand of the person next to you. I'll close our prayer after everyone in the circle has had a chance to pray.

WALL OF GRADUATES

COST: *$0*
WORK LEVEL: *moderate*
TIME INVOLVED: *short-term*
MATERIALS: *empty wall space, a list of young people who have recently graduated from your group, and tape or tacks*

Have you ever wished you could stay in touch with your graduating seniors as they go off to college or begin to work full-time? Have you ever wished your youth group could be in ministry to recent high school graduates? You can accomplish both. That's what the "wall of graduates" is all about.

The idea is simple. Place the names and addresses of college students and other recent graduates on a wall in the youth room (along with their pictures if you want). Tell your youth group members that each person can "adopt" a graduate and become a secret pal. All kids have to do is send anonymous letters of encouragement, small gifts, or e-mail messages from time to time. Then, at the end of the year, unite the graduates with their secret pals. This is a meaningful ministry, and everyone can benefit from the fun.

service project
Care Packages

THEMES: *love, unity*

MATERIALS: *large mailing envelopes (ten-by-thirteen-inches), a list of recent graduates and their addresses, pens, a variety of gift items, and Bibles*

Your youth group can reach out to graduates in a united service project. As a group, make "care packages" for college students and others who have recently graduated.

Encourage kids in your youth group to donate items for the care packages, such as pens, devotional booklets, local newspaper articles, stamps, candy, soap, bookmarks, self-stick notes, paper, gift certificates, and decorations. Be sure youth group members know that their donated items must fit in the mailing envelopes. You may also want to bring additional items in case group members don't bring enough.

Have your youth group members address the envelopes for mailing, stamp them, and stuff each one with gift items. You might also include a youth group newsletter, personal greetings, and a few selected Bible verses.

bonus idea

You might also want to send a nice note to the graduated students' parents. This is a great way to extend the ministry of the youth group to include the entire family.

WALL OF 'TOONS

COST: *$0-$10*

WORK LEVEL: *easy*

TIME INVOLVED: *short-term*

MATERIALS: *comic strips and tape or paintbrushes and paints and a blank wall*

If your young people love to laugh, you'll definitely want to begin a "wall of 'toons"—cartoons, that is. When I visited one youth room, I nearly laughed my head off as I read through hundreds of comic strips that teenagers had pasted on a long section of wall. The display was neat and clean and dealt primarily with religious and spiritual themes.

Another church painted original cartoon characters on a wall. Each cartoon featured a Bible verse or a quote as well as an autograph of the teenager who created the cartoon. The collection formed a wonderful inspiration of humor and faith.

You can make your wall of 'toons an ongoing project, or create it during an overnight retreat. Teenagers can bring in favorite cartoon ideas, clippings, or original drawings and then start painting or taping.

As you ponder the possibilities of painting cartoons in your youth room, I hope you'll remember that walls are recyclable. They can be painted again and again. If you don't like the way a wall turns out, you can always paint over it. Just keep laughing.

If you're taping comics to a wall, be sure to add new comics to your wall each week. Remove the older comics from time to time and replace them with new ones.

devotion

Lighthearted Lessons

THEME: *faith*
MATERIALS: *a large stack of comic strips and scissors (optional)*

This devotion idea never fails to produce a few laughs and some serious insights. You'll need a large stack of comic strips for this idea, which can take the place of a sermon or lesson or can encourage casual discussion. Sunday comic strips work best because they're in color and sometimes deal with religious themes. If you don't have a stack of comics you've saved, you can collect newspapers from church members and cut out the comic strip sections. Or if you're pressed for time, you may be able to get back issues of older newspapers at a small price from your local newspaper.

Have kids form a circle, and put your stack of comics in the center of the circle. Then say: **I'd like you to spend a few minutes looking through these comics. Choose one comic strip that teaches a lesson**

bonus idea

Bring in a book of some of your favorite Christian comic strip humor. *(The Adventures of...Jeremiah* and *Life at McPherson High* are some examples of favorite comic strips.)* Allow teenagers to borrow these. This will provide an opportunity for you to explain how you believe these comic strips use humor to address issues of faith.

about faith. Be prepared to tell the group about the comic strip and what you think we all can learn from it.

You might want to be prepared to help some teenagers who have difficulty grasping the concept, but most teenagers will embrace the idea handily. After a few minutes, give kids an opportunity to tell the group what they learned from their comic strips. Help students develop and explain their "lessons" as necessary. Encourage discussion and questions about the issues teenagers bring up. When each person has finished, encourage the rest of the group to clap for him or her.

After teenagers have presented their lessons, collect the comics and use them to start (or add to) your wall of 'toons.

PAINTED DOOR

COST: *$0-$25*
WORK LEVEL: *moderate*
TIME INVOLVED: *short-term*
MATERIALS: *assorted interior latex paints, masking tape, a drop-cloth, and paintbrushes*

The image of a doorway has always provided rich symbolism in Christian artwork. Much of this symbolism reflects the teachings of Jesus: "But when you pray, go into your room, close the door and pray to your Father, who is unseen" (Matthew 6:6a); "Knock and the door will be opened to you" (Matthew 7:7b); "I am the gate for the sheep" (John 10:7b).

As you think about Jesus' use of the door as a metaphor, think about the door to your youth area. Does the door beckon teenagers inside? Is it attractive? Dull? How well does it symbolize the invitation of Jesus? Can you envision making your door a work of Christian art?

Teenagers know how important doors are. They decorate their locker doors at school and hang posters on their bedroom doors at home. Why shouldn't they have a hand in decorating the door to the youth area?

Use paints and paintbrushes to do the work. Or, if you prefer something less permanent, try using posters, cutouts, and other decorations.

devotion

Behind Closed Doors

THEMES: *faith, prayer*

MATERIALS: *Bibles, index cards, pencils or pens, and a room with a door*

Leaving the door to your youth area open, give each person an index card and invite him or her to write down some prayer concerns. Stress that these concerns will be completely confidential.

Give each person a Bible, and invite teenagers to read Matthew 6:5-8 and Matthew 7:7-12. Then ask:

bonus idea

After members of your group have painted the door, hold an unveiling ceremony. Cover the door with butcher paper or wrapping paper, stretch a red ribbon across the front, and invite members of the congregation to be present for the cutting of the ribbon.

● What did Jesus teach about prayer in these passages?

● Why do you think Jesus stressed the importance of private prayer?

● What do you think Jesus meant when he said, "Knock and the door will be opened to you"?

● Where and when can you pray the best?

● How is faith connected with prayer?

Invite each teenager to make a private pledge concerning the amount of time he or she will spend in prayer each day. Ask the teenagers to write down on their index cards specific plans for times they intend to pray. Stress that they can take their index cards home and use them as reminders of their pledges.

As a symbolic act of entering into prayer, close the door to the youth area. Invite the teenagers to find their own quiet spaces in the room and pray for a few minutes for friends who are in trouble, for others in the group, and for themselves and their families.

When the prayer time is over, open the door.

NAME-TAG RACK

COST: *$50-$75*
WORK LEVEL: *moderate*
TIME INVOLVED: *long-term*
MATERIALS: *cork board or a plastic name-tag rack*

Not every youth group needs name tags, but if you happen to be in a church with a large youth program, you might want to consider a name-tag rack. This rack could be something as simple as a piece of cork board mounted on a wall (to hold pin-on name badges), or you could find a plastic rack at an office-supply store for less than $50 (these hold fifty to 100 of the clip-on name badges). Either way, if you have a large youth group, this is one way of helping teenagers and youth workers get to know each other by name.

I know other youth workers who have utilized name tags because of the eclectic nature of their groups—they may have teenagers who are from various high schools or teenagers who are vacationing in the area for a time. This can be especially true of churches located on the beach, near a tourist attraction, or close to an amusement park.

bonus idea

If you aren't certain whether you need permanent name tags or a rack in the youth room, try using stick-on name tags for a month. These don't cost much, and they'll give you a good idea of how well the teenagers like name tags and whether they believe permanent name-tags would be an asset to the group.

Remember—your name tags can be creative. Don't settle for plain paper printouts or handwritten names. Use some creative computer software to customize your own badges with logos, graphics, or clip art. If you want to, you can change the name tags each week with this type of software...at the click of a button.

Name tags also come in handy when you host larger youth events such as dances and concerts. This way you can identify even strangers by name and help create a feeling of friendship right away.

If you don't have plastic name-tags at your church, check an office-supply store. They should have a wide selection to choose from, and you should be able to outfit a group of 100 teenagers for less than $25.

What's in a Name?

THEMES: *the Bible, friendship, names*

MATERIALS: *Bibles, concordances, a Bible dictionary or a book of baby names (with meanings), and a list of Bible names (you can make up your own list or use the one below)*

Have kids form a circle and then ask:

● **Do any of you know someone who has a strange or unusual name?**

No doubt many of the teenagers will be able to relate a few stories of unusual or amusing names. (I personally have heard of a Harry Legg and a Penny Nichols, and I happened to see a tombstone with the name Ima Pigg.) Have fun sharing a few stories.

Give each person a Bible and a list of Bible names. Say: **Often we read a name in the Bible but fail to realize that names had a deep significance to people who lived long ago. Every name found in the Bible has a special meaning. Use your list, the concordances, and the Bible to find a Bible story about each person on your sheet. Then use the book of baby names or the Bible dictionary to discover the meaning of each name.**

Give each teenager time to work on his or her list individually, or have your group form teams and have a friendly competition. Allow the teenagers to relate what they discovered about the following biblical names:

● Adam   ● Gad   ● Jesus   ● Rachel
● Benjamin   ● Hosea   ● Joseph   ● Rebekah
● Eve   ● Jacob   ● Mary   ● Sarah
● Ezekiel   ● Moses

If time allows, use the baby book to look up the meaning of each teenager's name.

Food and Fun

POPCORN MACHINE

COST: *$200-$250*
WORK LEVEL: *easy*
TIME INVOLVED: *instant*
MATERIALS: *a "professional" popcorn machine, popcorn, oil, salt, and bowls or bags*

What ravenous teenager wouldn't like hot buttered popcorn—not the homemade type, but the mouthwatering morsels available only in movie theaters and sports arenas?

Finding a professional popcorn machine isn't difficult. Many large warehouse centers, retail clubs, and discount centers carry these machines for around $200. They're relatively easy to store, and they can be placed on rolling carts for easy mobility.

The popcorn machine can be a mainstay for each youth meeting, or it may be rolled out for special occasions such as seasonal kickoffs, Super Bowl parties, outreach events, lock-ins, and overnight meetings.

devotion
Popcorn Faith

THEMES: *change, spiritual growth*
MATERIALS: *a Bible, newsprint, a marker, tape or tacks, a professional popcorn machine, oil, butter, popcorn, salt, and bowls or bags*

Have teenagers form a circle, and ask:
● What ingredients are needed to make corn pop?

● What do you think would happen if any of those ingredients were missing?

● How do you think those ingredients work together to make corn pop?

41

Say: Without the ingredients of oil, moisture, and heat—in all the proper proportions—the popcorn kernel won't pop. A kernel won't be transformed into a tasty morsel.

Have a volunteer read Luke 17:6 aloud to the group. Then ask:

● What do you think Jesus was trying to tell his disciples about the nature of faith?

● When and how has a little faith made a difference in your life?

● How do you think faith works to change people's lives?

As teenagers answer, write their responses on a piece of newsprint. Then give each teenager a single popcorn kernel.

bonus idea

You may want to use this devotion and serve the popcorn at the beginning of a youth meeting.

Say: Take a look at how small this seed is. Jesus said that even a small amount of faith can produce big results. If you plant a seed, it will grow. If you give this kernel of corn the right environment, it will explode into something much larger and more useful. Likewise, if we allow God to use what little faith we have, it will grow. Every day can be a new experience of growth and challenge in our lives.

Encourage each person to look at the list you've written on newsprint and pick one item that reflects a kind of change he or she needs. Say: Think about how you'd like to see God use your faith to change you.

We'll be making a batch of popcorn today. As we do so, watch the marvelous transformation from seeds into fully popped kernels. Think about the change you'd like to see in your life, and pray that God will use your faith to transform you. Remember that faith changes things—relationships, habits, and desires.

As you close, allow teenagers to prepare the popcorn machine. Make a batch of popcorn, and add extra butter or salt. As the popcorn is popping, encourage teenagers to form a circle around the popcorn machine and spend several moments in silent prayer.

SODA FOUNTAIN

COST: *$100-$500*
WORK LEVEL: *easy*
TIME INVOLVED: *short-term*
MATERIALS: *an old-fashioned soda fountain or a name-brand soft drink dispenser and cups*

Even though today's teenagers are creatures of high-tech, computerized living, many still have a sense of nostalgia. And most teenagers have a seemingly endless appetite for soft drinks. What better way to appeal to that appetite and the sense of nostalgia than with a soda fountain?

If you think your teenagers might enjoy this feature, there are several ways you can go about setting up a soda fountain in your youth room. If you want a vintage soda fountain, try looking in antique malls. Many fountains from the '50s and '60s still exist, although you may have to fix them up a little. You should be able to find one of these fountains for under $500.

Another option, if you're looking for something a bit more modern, is to rent a name-brand soft drink dispenser. Just call your local soft drink distributor for prices. A soft drink company can set you up with a machine on a daily, monthly, or yearly basis. They'll even service the machine. All you have to provide are cups. Renting a soft drink dispenser might be an affordable option for your youth group, particularly if you have a large mob of thirsty teenagers.

If you're planning a major youth event, look into renting a soft drink dispenser for the event. You'll probably find that it will be less expensive than buying individual cans or liters.

discussion starter
Soft Drink Choices

THEME: *peer pressure*
MATERIALS: *a written list (or menu) for each teenager showing various soft drink flavors you have available*

Give each teenager a list of soft drink flavors, and invite kids to mingle while they make their selections. As kids are mingling, ask each person individually what flavor of soft drink he or she would like. Be sure to say to each person: **Of course, most people are choosing** (name one flavor). **Can I put you down for the same?**

After everyone has made a choice, have the group form a circle and ask:

● **How many of you chose** (name the flavor you suggested to everyone)?

Allow a show of hands and then ask:

● **Why did you choose that particular flavor?**
● **Were any of you influenced by my suggestion that everyone else was choosing that flavor? Why or why not?**
● **Were any of you influenced by the choices your friends made? Why or why not?**

Give each person the soft drink he or she requested, and have kids sit in a circle.

Begin a discussion of the influence of peer pressure on the lives of your students. Ask questions such as the following:

● Do you think it's easy to be different from others in our culture? Why or why not?

● How does a person's willingness to be different from others change from one situation to another?

● In what situations have you decided it's easier to go with the flow and be like everyone else?

● How does peer pressure affect your life (for better or for worse)?

● How do you think peer pressure affects the lives of people you know?

bonus idea

Once each person has chosen a soft drink flavor, have teenagers form groups based on their selections. Have fun with these choices by allowing the groups to make "sales pitches" to the other groups, attempting to convince others to switch preferences. After several minutes, see which flavor has the most support.

SNACK BAR

COST: *$25-$30*
WORK LEVEL: *easy*
TIME INVOLVED: *instant*
MATERIALS: *TV trays and snack foods*

Consider these two basic facts of youth ministry: Teenagers love to eat, and teenagers love to eat snack food. You can take advantage of these facts by setting up a simple snack bar in the youth room. Here's how.

Go to a yard- or garage-sale and find an inexpensive but nice-looking (of course!) set of TV trays. Set up the trays in one corner of the youth room before your meeting begins. Cover each tray with an assortment of snack foods such as chips and dips, cookies, and doughnuts. You may also want to include healthy snacks such as carrot sticks, celery, yogurt, bagels, and rice cakes. If you want your kids to think you have class, turn your TV trays into a sushi bar with tofu and raw fish!

The nice thing about these portable TV trays is that you can take them with you on the road to picnics, overnight events, road trips, and retreats. TV trays don't wear out easily, and they can hold a surprising amount of food.

devotion

Junk Food Faith?

THEMES: *faith, spiritual growth*
MATERIALS: *TV trays, assorted junk foods and healthy snack foods, Bibles, two pieces of poster board, and markers*

Give one group a collection of junk food such as chips, cookies, and candy. Give the other group some nutritious snack foods such as fruit juice, yogurt, and raw vegetables. Give each group a Bible, a piece of poster board, and markers.

Instruct each group to study the ingredients in each of its food items. Ask:

● **What can you tell me about the nutritional content of the foods I've given you?**

Allow time for teenagers from each group to respond and then ask:

Use the junk food and the nutritious snacks to start a discussion concerning the foods people would like to include in the snack bar. You might find that many teenagers prefer healthier snacks such as bagels, vegetables, and other low-fat items (at least some of the time).

● What makes some foods more nutritious than others?

● What would happen to our bodies if we ate only the foods I gave to the junk food group?

● What would happen to our bodies if we ate only the foods I gave to the nutritious food group?

● What does it take to have a strong and healthy body?

Have a volunteer from each group read 1 Timothy 4:6-10 aloud. Then ask:

● What do these verses say about being a strong and healthy person?

● What does it take to become spiritually fit?

Say: This Scripture passage reminds us that we need to be nourished in the faith. That means there are some things that help us grow spiritually and other things that can keep us from growing. Just as in the foods we eat, there are good spiritual ingredients and bad spiritual ingredients. I'd like one group to make a "top ten" list of "ingredients" that can help us to grow spiritually and the other group to make a "top ten" list of ingredients that can keep us from growing spiritually.

When each group has created a "top ten" list, have groups read their lists to the class. You may want to play up the drama by doing a "drum roll," playing music, or having kids do a "drum roll" before each item is read. After the lists have been read, read aloud 1 Timothy 4:6-10 again.

Post the "top ten" lists on the wall, and close with prayer.

CAPPUCCINO MACHINE

COST: *$100-$500*
WORK LEVEL: *easy*
TIME INVOLVED: *short-term*
MATERIALS: *a cappuccino machine, ground coffee, milk, and foam cups or mugs*

Many teenagers enjoy specialty coffees, especially cappuccino. An increasing number of churches are offering this frothy coffee drink in their fellowship areas on Sunday mornings, and I've seen a few machines in youth areas.

A cappuccino machine costs between $100 and $400 and can be moved easily. For this reason, a cappuccino machine is one item that everyone in the church can use. You might find that you can share the expense with other groups in the church.

If you want to see how a cappuccino machine would go over in your group, borrow a machine from a friend and note the response, or take a survey among the teenagers. During the winter, many young people and chaperones will enjoy a hot mug of frothy coffee as they enter the building. In fact, your group might make the cappuccino machine a gathering place for casual fellowship.

Be attentive to cappuccino choices—perhaps include both decaffeinated and regular. Or if you consider your teenagers too lively already, stick with decaffeinated only!

bonus idea

Take advantage of your Sunday-morning exposure to distribute information about your youth ministry—upcoming events, highlights, or mission opportunities. Not only will you educate the church about the young people and their ministries, but you might also pick up a few new volunteers or students.

service project

Cappuccino Greeters

THEMES: *servanthood, sharing*

MATERIALS: *a cappuccino machine, ground coffee, milk, mugs or foam cups, and a sign-up sheet*

Use the cappuccino machine for an easy service project. Make a sign-up sheet for teenagers to volunteer as worship greeters on Sunday mornings. In addition to welcoming guests and visitors, the teenagers can give people cups of cappuccino.

Service projects of this type on Sunday morning are a great way to call attention to the youth ministry of your church. The congregation gets to see the teenagers being involved.

FAST-FOOD BOOTHS

COST: *$200-$450 per booth*
WORK LEVEL: *difficult*
TIME INVOLVED: *long-term*
MATERIALS: *lumber, screws and nails, plastic for table tops, tools, and paint*

All fast-food chains have booths in their restaurants. Many people prefer booths to tables and chairs because booths offer more intimacy—more people can fit into a smaller space. Teenagers have grown accustomed to sitting in these booths for hours, sipping soft drinks and talking with friends. Why not use this type of seating arrangement to your advantage? Instead of having teenagers sit on the floor or in chairs, install some fast-food booths in your youth center.

The cost of having a contractor build and install these booths for you is rather expensive—at least $450 apiece for booths with plastic tops and seating for six. But most people know of experienced carpenters or wood-shop hobbyists who would be willing to help with a project in the youth room. An experienced carpenter can take measurements of booths at a local restaurant, purchase the materials you'll need, and construct the booths for less than half the cost of hiring an outside contractor.

If you manage to find the carpenters you need within your congregation, try to arrange a time when the teenagers in your group can help with the construction.

Having fast-food booths in your youth center can save you floor space—particularly if they replace tables and chairs—and they can also double as great small-group discussion areas.

Booth Bonanza

THEMES: *music, popular culture*

MATERIALS: *comic books, lists of scavenger hunt items (see "Comic Book Scavenger Hunt" or "CD Scavenger Hunt" below), CDs, loop-shaped breakfast cereal, cups, and spoons*

If you have a few booths in the youth room and you want some quiet games you can use with small groups, here are three that many teenagers will enjoy without the noise and high activity of other games.

Have kids form teams of four to six, and instruct one team to sit at each booth.

Comic Book Scavenger Hunt

Give each team a stack of comic books and a list of items to find (see the list below). If you want to, you can assign point values to each item, set a time limit, and have teams compete against each other. Include these items on your list:

- an advertisement for X-ray glasses
- an advertisement for a weight-loss product or gimmick
- a comic frame with no words inside
- a full-page frame
- a clock
- a watch
- a ring
- an explosion
- a word with more than twenty letters
- a super hero who doesn't wear a mask
- a rocket ship
- a picture of another planet
- a "help wanted" advertisement
- an advertisement for a surprise package

CD Scavenger Hunt

Give each team a dozen CDs and a list of items to find on the label or lyrics insert of the album. Include these items on your list:

- the word "love"
- the word "Jesus"

bonus idea

After playing the CD game, allow teenagers to select some of their favorite songs on the CDs you gave them. Play these songs in the background during the rest of your youth meeting. You might also use the cereal to make a snack.

- the phrase "Thank you, Mom and Dad."
- a picture of a guitar
- a picture of drums
- a picture of a car
- the word "O"
- a picture of an airplane
- the word "heaven"
- the word "God"
- a picture of a baby
- the word "baby"

Cereal Winks

Give each team approximately 100 pieces of loop-shaped breakfast cereal, a cup, and a spoon for each person. Although this is a sit-down game, it will make a mess because each team tries to be the first to flip twenty-five pieces of cereal into its cup (using only the spoons, of course). Holding a spoon in one hand, each person on a team can "load" the spoon with one piece of cereal and try to flip it into the cup. This is more difficult than it may seem.

Another option is to set a time limit for this game. The team with the most pieces of cereal in its cup at the end of play will be the winner.

MICROWAVE/REFRIGERATOR

COST: *$100-$500*
WORK LEVEL: *easy*
TIME INVOLVED: *instant*
MATERIALS: *a microwave oven (and a cart) and/or a refrigerator*

If you've ever wanted to save time and money on food for your group, a microwave and a refrigerator would help. A microwave will allow you to fix hot snacks quickly (or warm up leftover pizza), and a refrigerator will allow you to buy some items in larger quantities and keep leftovers, which can save money. And neither one takes up much space.

Microwaves sell for $100 to $150, and small refrigerators can be found for about the same price. Larger refrigerator/freezer units sell for $500 and up. And don't forget that you might find church members who would be willing to donate an old refrigerator, freezer, or microwave.

Microwave S'mores

THEMES: *none*

MATERIALS: *paper plates, large marshmallows, chocolate bars, graham crackers, napkins, and beverages*

On a paper plate, place one marshmallow and a piece of chocolate bar between two graham crackers. Microwave the snack for fifteen seconds on high (or until the chocolate and the marshmallow are lightly melted). Serve with milk, hot chocolate, or another beverage.

S'mores make great winter snacks and can be used to begin a meeting on a sweet note.

bonus idea

Along with making S'mores, invite the teenagers to bring in favorite microwaveable snack ideas and ingredients. Prepare a sign-up sheet, and invite volunteers to bring microwaveable snacks each week. Involve the teenagers in preparing these snacks for each meeting.

SNACK MACHINE

COST: *$0-$50 per month*
WORK LEVEL: *easy*
TIME INVOLVED: *long-term*
MATERIALS: *a rental snack-machine*

Many youth centers are located in areas where many people, not just teenagers, congregate or pass through. If you happen to have a youth room located in a high-traffic area, you might consider getting a snack machine for the area. These machines can be rented or purchased. They can also be consigned by a vending company in your area if you have enough volume. In this situation, the company will take care of the upkeep of the machine and the collection of the money. Your youth group would get a portion of the profits.

Most of these machines can be rented for around $50 per month, and a balance of junk foods and more healthy snacks can be placed in the racks.

One advantage to having this kind of machine near a youth area is that you might not have to worry about snacks or drinks each time you have a youth meeting. If you find that you're spending a lot of time worrying about food and drinks for each meeting, this might work well for you (particularly if you have a large group). Not only would the machines save you time, but they would also be a built-in fund-raiser.

If you're considering a snack machine for your youth area, call several local snack or candy companies in your area. They can be found in the Yellow Pages under Food Service Distributors or Food Service Management.

group builder

Candy Corps

THEMES: *cooperation, responsibility*
MATERIALS: *ballots or slips of paper and pencils*

bonus idea

You can change your candy-corps leaders every year by taking an annual vote, with the winning people assuming their new responsibilities on a specific date. This allows the positions of leadership to pass from teenager to teenager. Young people can also learn more about cooperation. Or if you prefer, have one class (such as eleventh-graders) ➜

Once you've decided to get a snack machine, have fun with the concept by involving everyone in your group.

One way to involve students is to assign each of them to serve on one of three candy-corps teams. One team will be responsible for calling food distributors in your area, gathering prices and brochures about services, and reporting the team's recommendations to the whole group. The second team will be responsible for working with the church board to find a suitable location for the machine, answering questions, and assisting in the setup. The third team will be responsible for monitoring the snack machine, making sure it's filled each week, and trouble-shooting any problems.

Another option for involving teenagers is to allow them to select the snacks and candies for the machine. If you're renting the machine or you have

take responsibility for maintaining the machine. Each year, you'll start over with a new group of teenagers. it on consignment, most distributors will give you a list of goods that can be included inside the machine. Use this master list to make up a survey, give each group member a chance to vote, tally the scores, and report the results.

To have a bit more fun with the process, make your voting procedure like a political campaign. Form two or more political parties (each can choose a name based on the types of snacks it would like to support), sponsor debates among the elected speakers for each party, and then take a vote and report your results. The winning party can be responsible for the upkeep and maintenance of the machine.

VIDEO GAMES

COST: *$20-$250*
WORK LEVEL: *difficult*
TIME INVOLVED: *long-term*
MATERIALS: *rental arcade games, television game cartridges and a game system, or CD-ROM games and a computer with a CD-ROM drive*

Today's teenagers are certainly a video game-oriented generation. They play video games at mall arcades, at amusement parks, at home, and even at school. They have games for computers and television, three-dimensional and virtual reality games, and hand-held games. They play old pinball games and new games on cartridge and CD-ROM.

I've seen more and more youth centers taking advantage of this game craze. A few youth centers have made an effort to draw kids off the streets by offering video arcades inside the church. Some of these arcade games are older units that have been phased out over the years. These "antique" video games can be rented through local game-distributors, or you might be able to purchase them outright for far less than the newer games. Video game vendors can be found in the Yellow Pages, or you can obtain phone numbers for the companies by visiting an arcade in your area and jotting down the toll-free numbers listed on the game consoles.

If you don't want to worry about full-size arcade games, you may want to purchase a television game-system. These cartridge systems sell for $200-$250. Individual game cartridges are $20-$40.

A third option, if you already have a computer in the youth room, is to utilize the CD-ROM. CD-ROM games cost $20-$50 and come in a variety of genre, such as adventure, educational, and fantasy. You might want to preview anything you're thinking about purchasing.

If you're thinking about having video games in the youth center, you'll want to carefully consider all the positives and negatives. For example, if you're trying to attract teenagers who might otherwise hang out on the streets, video games might bring them inside the church. You'll want to have the newest games you can afford, though, and you'll also have to have plenty of adult supervision. If you're wanting to provide a place for teenagers to gather after school events or even before youth meetings, a video center might become a social center for these young people. Remember, though, that the games will have to be monitored, and you'll need a definite plan for fitting these games into your overall youth ministry. You won't want your kids hanging out at the video center when they should be in youth meetings.

As with anything, there are positive and negative aspects to this idea. Many churches have done a nice job of taking a balanced approach and including this type of recreation in their youth rooms.

outreach project
Arcade Helpers

THEMES: *outreach, peer counseling, service*
MATERIALS: *a video arcade for young people*

I spoke with one youth leader who utilized a video arcade (made up primarily of pinball machines) in an outreach program in his youth ministry. Every Friday night a group of people from the church would show up to monitor the video arcade. Volunteers from the youth group were also trained to help with the activities in the arcade. Some of these Friday-night activities included welcoming new teenagers, getting names and addresses of new teenagers for the youth group mailing list, organizing games, and conducting brief devotions.

This youth group definitely used the video arcade as a mission opportunity. Their primary focus was helping move teenagers off the streets and into an environment of care and support where they could be introduced to faith in Jesus.

If you set up a video arcade for young people, you may want to plan to include crowdbreaker activities, space for kids to sit down and talk, brief outreach-oriented devotions, and other opportunities for social interaction. Try to make your arcade into more than a place to play games—make it a place where meaningful relationships can form.

Organizing your teenagers to participate in this type of peer activity can be rewarding in many ways. Teenagers may grow to understand what it means to be a leader, gain valuable outreach experience, and grow in their self-assurance and self-esteem. If you have an opportunity to reach out to teenagers in the community through this type of ministry, organizing your own youth group to help might be an important step.

This type of outreach activity can be a real team-builder for your group, and you might be able to make an important impact on your community.

bonus idea

If you decide to create your own church video-arcade, be sure to provide training sessions for those teenagers who volunteer to help. Teenagers, like adults, appreciate support and preparation. Role playing and talking about possible difficult situations will help teenagers be prepared for these situations if they occur.

TELESCOPE

COST: *$300-$400*
WORK LEVEL: *easy*
TIME INVOLVED: *short-term*
MATERIALS: *a telescope*

Psalm 19 begins with these words: "The heavens tell the glory of God, and the skies announce what his hands have made." Indeed the heavens are wondrous and beautiful. And stargazing with a high-powered telescope can be a great way to remember the majesty and power of God.

The first time I peered at the moon through a telescopic lens, I was amazed at the stark contrast of details—the depth of the white-rimmed craters, the shadows of mountains, the dark lines of crevices and ravines, the luminous brightness of the sun's reflection on the moon's surface. And I was amazed to learn that most of the stars I could see with the naked eye were actually clusters of stars, galaxies, or planets.

The good news is that buying a powerful telescope doesn't have to break your bank account. A telescope with a four-and-a-half-inch aperture mirror and a tracking device (a feature that allows for the rotation of the earth) can be purchased for around $300. Less powerful telescopes don't cost as much, but the decline in quality is definitely noticeable. If your youth group is interested in a telescope, I suggest that you look at larger models and, if your budget is anemic, figure out a way to pay for one.

A telescope makes a fine addition to any outdoor retreat, campout, or special event. Astronomy guidebooks are also available. These books can help you understand the arrangement of constellations and the names of major stars.

Once you have your telescope, you'll be able to observe the universe with a new sense of awe and affirm with the psalmist, "Day after day they pour forth speech; night after night they display knowledge" (Psalm 19:2).

devotion

Creation Collection

THEME: *the Bible, creation*
MATERIALS: *flashlights and a Bible*

Use your telescope as the centerpiece in this study of God's creation. Begin the study by allowing teenagers to take turns gazing through the telescope at constellations or galaxies. As teenagers look through the telescope, have a volunteer read slowly from Genesis 1. After the reading, have kids form a circle and allow them to respond to these questions:

● What new insights about God have you gained from looking at the stars?

● Does looking at distant galaxies make God seem closer to you, or more distant? Why?

bonus idea

If you know someone who is knowledgeable in astronomy, invite him or her to point out to your youth group some of the more impressive constellations.

56

Instruct teenagers to form groups of four to six. Give each group at least one flashlight and then say: **I'd like each group to search for something that reminds you of God's creative power. For example, you might find a flower, an insect, or some other object that is a reminder of God's creation. Bring the object back to the group, and be ready to explain why it's significant.**

Give the teenagers a time limit of several minutes, and tell them where to meet. Be sure each group has at least one watch. When everyone has returned, allow each group to share its object with the others, explaining why it chose the object it did.

When each group has shared, have kids form a circle and put their objects in the middle of the circle. Offer prayers of thanks for God's creation. Read aloud Psalm 19.

INDOOR CHALLENGE-COURSE

COST: *$0*
WORK LEVEL: *easy*
TIME INVOLVED: *short-term*
MATERIALS: *cardboard-box tops, old rugs, or used doormats; three donated two-by-fours; and masking tape*

Challenge courses are exciting team-builders. These courses, usually consisting of wires and ropes strategically secured among trees, are designed for physical challenge, but they also engage the emotions and the intellect. Many of these challenge courses are top-notch creations of professional engineers and shouldn't be imitated by amateurs. It would be unwise and unsafe to attempt to construct an elaborate challenge-course among trees or rocks without proper engineering and supervision.

But youth groups can construct other types of challenge courses that are safe, simple, and inexpensive. These courses can be constructed indoors in a short time.

Here are two challenge-courses your group might find enjoyable and exciting. Use these ideas as a springboard for your own fun and practical creations.

Steppingstones

Before teenagers arrive, arrange a series of cardboard-box tops, rugs, or mats on the floor. These are the "steppingstones"—the only places the teenagers may walk. Arrange the steppingstones in such a way that the teenagers will be challenged to help each other across the maze of stones.

When kids arrive, instruct kids to find a way to get everyone from one side of the course to the other. Everyone is on the same team, so this is not a competition. The goal is for the members of the group to find a way to work together to get everyone in the group "safely" to the other side without falling into the "water."

Those who fall into the water must go back to the beginning of the course (with encouragement from the group) and begin again. This makes a great team-builder because, as opposed to personal competition, the goal is for the group to accomplish this feat together.

For an added challenge, make some of the stones higher by placing them on crates, stools, or furniture. Make other stones unusually small, squishy, or misshapen. You might also create your own set of rules for the challenge course (such as setting a time limit, limiting the number of teenagers per stone, or having the teenagers proceed through the stones in the course in a certain order).

Two-by-Four Challenge

This challenge course is simple to make but difficult to defeat. You'll need three two-by-fours, masking tape, and a bit of imagination.

Begin by marking two boundaries on the floor with the masking tape at least thirteen feet apart. The object of the challenge course is for the teenagers to walk across the two-by-fours from one boundary line to the other. They'll be able to accomplish this feat only by helping each other walk across the narrow boards without falling off. You'll also want to encourage students to hold the boards steady for each other so the boards don't slide. Anyone who steps off the boards must return to the beginning of the course, so balance is important.

bonus idea

Keep track of how quickly your group was able to complete each challenge course. Encourage your group to try from time to time to break its personal record. This will excite everyone to strive toward a goal together, and you will certainly hear your teenagers cheering each other on as they get closer to breaking their own record.

To begin the game, the teenagers must decide the best way to arrange the boards to help span the distance between the boundaries. If necessary, remind them that they can't step on the floor between the two boundaries. Teenagers must work together to figure out the best way to get everyone from one side to the other.

Use this challenge course to build confidence and trust within the entire group. Stronger, more agile teenagers must learn to help those who are not as athletic or those who might feel less confident in their abilities to walk on a narrow board. Students with physical disabilities might require everyone's help. Everyone is on the same team, striving for the same objective and cheering each other on.

In challenge courses, the whole group wins, and there are no losers. These courses can really boost the love and unity within a group.

discussion starter

Community Challenge

THEMES: *the body of Christ, community*
MATERIALS: *a Bible*

After completing one of the challenge courses above (or one of your own invention), use this discussion starter to talk about the meaning of Christian community. Begin by reading Romans 15:14.

Ask:

● What did you learn about yourself by completing this challenge course?

● What did you learn about our group?

● How would you describe our group at this point?

● How can we support each other even better?

● What does Christian community mean?

● How might we understand this Scripture passage in light of the challenge course we just completed?

Close the discussion with a group hug or cheer.

Learning Options

BOOKSTORE

COST: *$0-$100 per year*
WORK LEVEL: *moderate*
TIME INVOLVED: *long-term*
MATERIALS: *shelving or a storage area for books, and books*

Most teenagers will read helpful books on issues such as sex, peer pressure, and relationships. Whenever I visit a bookstore, I'm amazed at the number of teenagers who are browsing the stacks or buying magazines.

Having a bookstore in the youth room might be one way of drawing teenagers into the world of reading by providing positive reading material. Books can provide a wealth of helpful information and can inspire teenagers to live more honestly, creatively, or faithfully. Many teenagers would welcome the opportunity to purchase devotional guides and gift books in the youth room.

Setting up a bookstore can be quite easy—especially if earning a profit is inconsequential. One way is to purchase several books that teenagers might want to buy and then sell them at the same price as you bought them. If you have something more substantial in mind, you may want to talk to a local bookseller and see if he or she might set up a consignment agreement for your youth room bookstore.

If you decide to set up a bookstore for your youth group, you can involve teenagers in selling books, keeping inventory, and stocking shelves.

bonus idea

Your bookstore doesn't have to be grandiose or even in a permanent space. It might be a cardboard box, a row of shelves, or a library cart. A small shelf and equipment to hang it can be purchased for less than $40. You can assign some teenagers to make sure the bookstore is run properly.

Bookstore Questionnaire

THEMES: *cooperation, teamwork*
MATERIALS: *questionnaires and pens or pencils*

One way to set up a successful bookstore is to involve the teenagers in the initial decision-making process. Ask for their help in collecting an initial inventory of books that teenagers might like to buy. You can do this by having your group fill out the photocopiable questionnaire on page 63.

Using this questionnaire should give you a sample of the types of books you might want to sell in your bookstore. Once you have the bookstore established, involve the teenagers in keeping it stocked.

VIDEO-RENTAL CENTER

COST: *$100-$250 per year*
WORK LEVEL: *easy*
TIME INVOLVED: *long-term*
MATERIALS: *videotapes of movies and music and a storage unit for videotapes*

Since the advent of the videotape, many youth leaders have used this medium as a teaching resource. In fact, there are dozens of Christian companies that develop and sell videos specifically designed for youth groups, Christian education classes, and worship. Most of these are high-quality products that come packaged in designer sets and address a host of hot topics that teenagers find interesting. Using Christian-video services is one way to build a video library for the youth room.

Another way to build a video library is to purchase your own set of uplifting movies and music videos that teach lessons about living, loving, and learning. Video stores abound, and most retail stores have video tapes priced at $10 to $40. With a little money, you can soon build an impressive video library. Parents can help you organize the collection, and they might donate favorite family

Please check all the types of books you might be interested in buying if they were for sale at youth group.

❏ Devotion guides for teenagers
❏ Books about dating, sex, and relationships
❏ Books for high school graduates
❏ Christian novels
❏ Books that talk about contemporary issues
❏ Books that teach you more about Christianity
❏ Books that help you deal with problems your friends face
❏ Bible-study tools and helps
❏ Other (please specify) _____

List five topics that interest you:
1.
2.
3.
4.
5.

List five writers you enjoy:
1.
2.
3.
4.
5.

If books were available for purchase at youth group, how often would you be interested in buying one?

movies as a way of cutting costs.

Once you have a small collection, you can rent your videos for $1 apiece and use the money to purchase other movies in the future. A videotape cabinet or storage unit can be as simple as a crate or as fancy as a rotating unit designed specifically for videotapes.

One legal note: It's important to be aware that if you purchase a videotape, you may not show it at any gathering where teenagers or adults pay a registration cost. If, for any reason, you'll be charging your audience to attend—at a workshop or seminar, for example—you must have written permission to show the video. In other words, you can rent or buy a video and show it to your youth group, but you cannot charge an admission fee to view a videotape.

If you prefer to build a video library without the hassle of handling money, build a video library instead of a rental center. Allow students to check out videotapes and return them later.

Use your own creativity and good judgment as you build a video library for teenagers. It can serve as a great resource for your ministry. Videos can provoke strong feelings in teenagers and lead to lively discussions and marvelous insights.

devotion

Return to Oz

THEMES: *faith, heaven*

MATERIALS: *a videotape of* The Wizard of Oz, *a TV, a VCR, and a Bible*

Cue a videotape of *The Wizard of Oz* to a scene near the end of the movie—the scene in which Dorothy and her trio of friends have returned to the Wizard of Oz with the broom of the Wicked Witch. Begin to watch the movie at this point—the scene is about fifteen minutes long.

When the movie ends, ask:

● In what ways did Dorothy and her friends each receive what he or she had desired from the wizard?

● What did each character learn about himself or herself? about the others?

Have the teenagers form groups of three to five. Invite each teenager to share with his or her group a story of an unexpected gift he or she has received or

bonus idea

As you watch *The Wizard of Oz,* use some of the other projects outlined in this book. For example, you might utilize the popcorn machine, the cappuccino machine, or the snack bar.

a blessing that came about as a result of perseverance or faith. Allow groups about ten minutes for this activity.

When everyone has had a chance to tell a story, have teenagers discuss these questions in their groups:

- How do we learn to be wise? brave? loving?
- What does "home" mean to you?

Once the teenagers have responded to these questions, gather the entire group back together. Have volunteers take turns reading 2 Corinthians 5:1-10 aloud, one verse at a time. Then ask:

- What does this Scripture passage tell us about our eternal home?
- What other insights does this Scripture passage give you about our future with God?
- What should "home" mean to a Christian?
- What can the movie *The Wizard of Oz* teach us about faith?

PARENTS' CORNER

COST: *$0*
WORK LEVEL: *moderate*
TIME INVOLVED: *short-term*
MATERIALS: *one of the following items: empty wall space, a bulletin board, a corner of the room, a table, or a shelf*

One sure way to strengthen any youth group is to get parents involved. A unique way of getting parents involved is to provide them with a space in the youth room. This space can be a wall, a bulletin board, a corner of the room, a table, or a shelf—any area where parents can show their support through letters, pictures, or other symbols of encouragement.

This corner can also function as a place where parents sign up to be chaperones, drivers, or helpers. They can also sign up to take turns bringing meals or snacks to the youth meetings.

Another option is to provide a space for parents to do some creative sharing and teaching. I've seen an area that featured a parents' newsletter. Another had a "top ten" list of things parents wished they had known when they were teenagers. Some of these

bonus idea

You might want to invite a parent or parents to lead a youth discussion on a topic of their choice. Many parents are experts on issues they would like to address in a formal setting. This could provide a great opportunity for them to be involved in a meaningful way and for your teenagers to gain valuable insight.

items were poignant reminders that parents have made mistakes too. Parents and other adults can pass along valuable knowledge and advice to teenagers.

One of the most creative parents' corners I've seen featured a directory of phone numbers (in case teenagers ever needed rides home from parties, found themselves in trouble, or needed to discuss difficult issues with adults other than their own parents). This directory also featured the occupations of the adults in the church. Teenagers were invited to talk to any adults about their career choices as they approached graduation from high school.

A parents' corner in the youth room can also emphasize that youth ministry is more than just ministry to teenagers. Youth ministry involves the entire family and even the entire church community. Everyone can play a role in helping young people.

special event

Parent Night

THEMES: *communication, family*

MATERIALS: *invitations, food for a meal or snacks, and other supplies as determined by the activities you choose for this meeting*

Use this guide to organize a "Parent Night" youth meeting. After sending out written invitations to parents, follow up with phone calls, inviting parents for an evening of fun and learning. You might want to give each parent a special job to do, or treat the parents to a relaxed night *without responsibilities!*

As teenagers and parents arrive, provide a few opening crowd-breakers and a meal or a snack. Then have the parents and teenagers form groups for some relay games, challenge games (such as a Bible-trivia game), or other interactive fun.

As the main part of your meeting, hold a worship experience with plenty of singing. Read 1 John 2:12-14 and then form two discussion panels (one made up of teenagers and one made up of parents). Invite people on the panels to ask or respond to questions such as these:

- What does this Scripture passage teach us about relationships?
- What does God desire from us as families?
- According to this Scripture passage, how do you think God strengthens us to live as parents and teenagers in today's world?
- How do you think parents and teenagers can better communicate with each other?
- What barriers seem to exist between generations?
- Is there a generation gap? If so, how does it affect the way we relate to each other?
- What can parents do to help teenagers?
- What can teenagers do to help parents?
- What are some projects teenagers and parents can work on together?

After this discussion, close this portion of the meeting with prayer.

Use the rest of the youth meeting for interactive games. Record any ideas parents and teenagers shared during the meeting, and plan to use a few of them as ideas for upcoming meetings.

AFFIRMATION GRAFFITI

COST: *$25-$30*
WORK LEVEL: *easy*
TIME INVOLVED: *short-term*
MATERIALS: *empty wall space and paints and paintbrushes or spray paint*

At a youth-leaders seminar, I talked with a young woman who had taught her inner city teenagers how to make "affirmation graffiti." Affirmation graffiti, she said, came about as a result of working with local politicians who were trying to inhibit the spray-painting of walls. This had become a major problem in areas where gangs were prevalent.

Her youth group wanted to make a difference. Working with the mayor's office, her group of teenagers began to paint over these walls, transforming them into positive signs of God's peace and love. Teenagers used these walls to create affirming messages of hope.

Try to give your youth group a broader perspective on society and the body of Christ. If you live in a rural or suburban neighborhood, invite an inner city group to be part of your meeting. If you live in an inner city area, invite a group from the suburbs or a rural area. Or invite a group from another Christian denomination or a different Christian background and culture. Through this invitation you might help break down a few barriers of race, class, or denomination. Affirmation graffiti is an excellent way for teenagers to express their concern for each other.

This became a learning experience as well. Teenagers were given an opportunity to talk to local officials about youth issues and concerns. The political officials took the time to respond to these concerns and to offer workable solutions.

Naturally this idea can be adapted to fit your own situation. You can use affirmation graffiti in your youth room. Perhaps you have an ugly green wall that is just dying to be spray-painted. Work with your teenagers to create a unique work of modern art, or perhaps allow your teenagers to simply have fun by spray-painting a few Bible verses or words of affirmation on the wall. Be sure to ventilate the area and require students to wear protective masks when they paint.

Love Handles

THEMES: *fellowship, love*

MATERIALS: *butcher paper, paints and paintbrushes or markers, masking tape, and a Bible*

In case you don't have a spare wall in your youth room, affirmation graffiti can be created on butcher paper. All you need is a strip of butcher paper, some paints and paintbrushes or markers, and masking tape.

Unroll the butcher paper, distribute the markers or paints and brushes, and then say: **Today we're going to practice kindness, gentleness, and encouragement—which are signs of our love for each other. First, find a place on the butcher paper and write your name. Then I'd like you to use the markers** (or paints) **to write affirmation graffiti. These affirmations about each other can be signs, symbols, or words. Try to write something nice about each person in our group—something you appreciate about the person, something you admire, or something you enjoy.**

Allow adequate time for the teenagers to complete their affirmations. Tape the butcher paper to the wall, and read Philippians 4:8-9 aloud. Close with a group hug.

LIBRARY

COST: *$100-$250 per year*
WORK LEVEL: *difficult*
TIME INVOLVED: *long-term*
MATERIALS: *shelving, books, magazines, videotapes, cassettes, and CDs*

Over the years I've seen many youth rooms containing a wide selection of books, magazines, videotapes, cassettes, and CDs for teenagers. Most of these libraries were small collections with an emphasis on devotional materials, self-help books, and contemporary Christian music. Some also included Bible-study helps.

Like a bookstore, a library can be a source of help for many teenagers who don't know how or where to look for a book. Many public libraries don't carry a wide selection of religious books, and bookstores often don't shelve devotionals for teenagers.

Another popular item in youth group libraries is magazines. There are now dozens of fine Christian magazines devoted to teenage life and questions. Try subscribing to a few of these and making them available in your library. Many teenagers will also check out music cassettes, CDs, and videos. If they like them, they may want to purchase these items.

Establishing a good library doesn't have to be extremely difficult. You can start off by buying a few books and tapes, and expand year by year. Periodically you can sell off the older books and tapes that seem to have run through their popularity and use the money to buy new items. In a few years, you can take an empty shelf or two and transform it into a space teenagers will love to peruse before and after youth meetings. And be sure to involve teenagers in selecting materials and maintaining the library.

group builder

The Story of Our Lives

THEMES: *faithfulness, memories*
MATERIALS: *a hardcover historical ledger and old photographs from youth events*

bonus idea

You can use the completed ledger for a teaching moment. Ask:
● Why is it important to remember the past?
● What can we learn from people who have experienced life before us?
Read Psalm 44:1-3. Ask:
● What did the people of Israel remember about their ancestors?
● Who are our ancestors? →

Have you ever considered making a historical archive for the youth group? Have you ever wished you could pass along those special group moments or record them for future generations?

Here's a quick and easy way to make a historical record book for your group. You'll need to purchase a hardcover historical ledger (about $30); collect photographs from past youth trips, outings, and retreats; and organize information about past youth groups, leaders, and special events. This may take a bit of research or interviews with some of the older members of the congregation. Remember to involve your teenagers too. They can bring in pictures, recollections, and memorabilia from older siblings, parents, or grandparents who helped with the youth group in the past. From this collection, you should

• What events in our youth group should we remember when we give thanks to God?

• As you look through our youth group historical record, what people or events strike you as being particularly important? Why? Close by thanking God for the past and asking God's blessings on the future of your youth group.

be able to form an exciting historical record.

Invite your teenagers to participate in the making of this historical record. Each week, devote ten to fifteen minutes to working on the history of your group, or organize a special retreat for this task.

Paste photos and written memories into the ledger, allowing some space to make future additions. Keep the ledger in your youth-room library and add to it each year. Assign one of the teenagers to be the youth group historian. It will be his or her task to be responsible for making a year-end addition to the historical ledger. Appoint or elect a new youth group historian each year.

QUESTION-AND-ANSWER JARS

COST: *$0*
WORK LEVEL: *easy*
TIME INVOLVED: *long-term*
MATERIALS: *two jars or oatmeal boxes*

A few years ago I was given a set of "Question and Answer" jars as a gift. One jar had the word "Questions" on it. The other was labeled "Answers." These empty jars have always been a source of conversation when people enter my office and wonder what's inside them. For a while, I displayed the jars in the youth room, only to discover one day that they had been stuffed full of papers.

If you'd like to try this idea with your teenagers, use jars or a couple of oatmeal boxes. Label one "Questions" and the other "Answers." Leave the question-and-answer jars in the youth room for a while. Then after a few months, look inside and see what you find.

These jars can also be used to kick off discussion about a specific topic. Invite teenagers to drop their questions about that specific topic into the "Questions" jar. Do this for a couple of weeks, and then remove the questions, number them, and post them in a visible place in the youth room.

Next, allow teenagers to respond to the questions themselves by stuffing answers into the "Answers" jar, with their answers numbered to correspond with the appropriate questions. You're certain to get a few laughs, but you'll also get some great insights. Teenagers often feel less inhibited when they're offering written responses rather than spoken ones.

service project
Peer Counseling

THEMES: *leadership, love, outreach, peer counseling*
MATERIALS: *question-and-answer jars, slips of paper, and pencils*

Use question-and-answer jars as a way of helping teenagers be good peer counselors. Here's how.

At the beginning of one meeting, invite teenagers to drop anonymous questions into the "Questions" jar. These questions can pertain to faith issues, sexuality, drugs, peer pressure, or any other topic. Quickly review the questions to make sure they're appropriate and then number them and return them to the jar.

bonus idea

If conversation with peers is too intimidating for kids, publish a few of the questions and answers in your newsletter. This feature could become a regular column.

At the end of the meeting, invite each teenager to draw a question from the "Questions" jar. Invite each person to take the question home, think about it, and prepare an anonymous written response for next week. Tell kids to number their answers to correspond to the appropriate question.

At the next meeting, have kids drop their answers into the "Answers" jar as they enter the room. Read the answers to make certain they're appropriate. During the meeting, read the questions and the corresponding answers, or let kids draw questions and read the appropriate answers. Teenagers can use the question-and-answer jars for ongoing conversations with peers.

MAGAZINE RACK

COST: *$15-$100*
WORK LEVEL: *easy*
TIME INVOLVED: *instant*
MATERIALS: *a magazine rack and subscriptions to several magazines*

Perhaps you can't afford to have a library (p. 69) or a bookstore (p. 61) in your youth area. But you can probably find space and a budget for a magazine rack (most retail for around $15) and a few magazine subscriptions for teenagers (around $20 per year per magazine). Consider all the fine magazines that are available for teenagers today. In additional to your denominational youth magazine, take a look at some of the magazines in Christian bookstores. There are many for teenagers, and most deal with timely issues in a well-rounded and informative manner. Buy a few samples, take them back to the youth room, and see how your teenagers respond.

If your experience shows you that a magazine rack would go over big with your teenagers, try to find a rack that will display four to six stacks of magazines at a glance.

At times you can find used magazine-racks at library sales or stores that advertise "going out of business" sales. Sometimes you can find wonderful racks at discount prices.

Once you have a large supply of magazines, either issue the volumes on a take-and-return basis or use some type of checkout system.

bonus idea

In addition to keeping Christian youth magazines on hand, you might want to expand your selection to include magazines such as National Geographic, Biblical Archaeology Review, and a few decent computer magazines. These magazines contain articles that could also inform, enlighten, and provoke discussion.

discussion starter

Dateline

THEMES: *dating, relationships, sexuality*
MATERIALS: *magazines for teenagers*

Invite the group to peruse the stack of youth magazines for articles pertaining to dating or sexuality. Give each person a few minutes to locate

Look through the magazines on your rack, and make a list of articles your teenagers might find helpful or interesting. You might want to categorize these articles under headings like "School," "Sex," "Smoking," "Drugs," "Abuse," "Dating," and so forth. Update the list from time to time. Use some of these categories to find articles that will serve as discussion starters for other subjects.

an article. Then invite each teenager to read one or two paragraphs from the article he or she found.

Begin a discussion about dating and sexuality by asking these questions:

● What is the author trying to say about dating or sexuality? Do you agree or disagree? Explain.

● What aspect of dating or sexuality do you wish someone would write about?

● What's the most important thing to keep in mind when on a date?

● What biblical principles are mentioned in your article?

● What does your article say about sexuality in dating relationships? Do you agree? Why or why not?

After discussing one or more of these questions, consider using one of the articles as a springboard to a lesson on dating or sexuality.

DISCUSSION BOX

COST: *$0-$5*
WORK LEVEL: *easy*
TIME INVOLVED: *instant*
MATERIALS: *a homemade container or an index-card file, index cards, and pencils*

Ever had one of those weeks when you were unprepared to lead a youth meeting? One way to alleviate this frustration is to have a "discussion box" in the youth center—a small box filled with hot topics and lively themes. On those days (hopefully they're rare) when you just have to grab for the salvation of the discussion box, it will be only an arm's length away. Use the discussion box sparingly, and you'll be sure to have a host of top-notch topics at your disposal.

A small cardboard box will work well. If you prefer something more substantial and upscale, use an index-card file. It won't take you long to rig up something.

Once you have your discussion box, don't hesitate to involve the teenagers in helping you prepare the topics. From time to time, ask your kids to write down discussion topics on index cards and drop these into the discussion box. The teenagers can also include concerns and questions they would like to talk about.

Topics Galore

THEMES: *none*

MATERIALS: *discussion box, newspapers and magazines, scissors, index cards, and pencils or pens*

Distribute newspapers and magazines. Invite the teenagers to cut out articles or pictures that represent topics they would like to discuss. Make a big mound of these topics and then begin to divide them into various piles according to theme or subject matter.

Then ask the teenagers to sort through the various piles and create questions pertaining to each topic—one question per index card. For example, there may be several newspaper and magazine articles about poverty. These articles could translate into questions such as "What can the church do to alleviate poverty?" or "Is there any way our youth group could work in a soup kitchen?" Articles about teenage pregnancy might translate into questions like "Is it all right to have sex before marriage if you use a condom?" or "What does the Bible say about sex?"

Instruct the teenagers to write these questions on their index cards and alphabetize them in the discussion box according to subject matter. Involving the group in this way will prepare the discussion box with dozens of ready-to-go topics.

bonus idea

After you've prepared the discussion box, pull out one or two of the questions and see where they lead. You may find that the teenagers are more willing to discuss controversial topics than you ever imagined they would be.

Multimedia

COMPUTER

COST: *$1600 and up*
WORK LEVEL: *easy*
TIME INVOLVED: *short-term*
MATERIALS: *a computer with a CD-ROM drive and preloaded software*

In this day and age, can a youth room really be complete without a computer? The next generation of teenagers will be more heavily influenced by computer technology than any other generation. Children who are learning how to use computers in grade school will have a deep and abiding interest in software, programs, and computer games—count on it.

An increasing number of churches are setting up computers in their youth areas. Thousands of churches are now online, and in many respects, the church has become a viable presence on the World Wide Web. There are Christian chat rooms, a wealth of information (everything from sermon illustrations to Bible translations), and a variety of web pages—all to be found on the Internet.

No doubt the future will hold many surprises for those churches that venture into cyberspace. In the next decade we'll see the advent of even bolder technologies that will enable the church to reach out to and communicate with teenagers, children, and the world community—all through the use of computers.

If you're considering a computer for your youth area, hold your breath. Computers aren't cheap. A basic computer with a CD-ROM drive and multimedia capabilities begins at around $1600. However, prices continue to fall as technology and computer capabilities rise. The only problem is that the moment you buy a computer, it's nearly obsolete—computers are changing that rapidly.

A less expensive option is to buy a computer from a company that builds computers from old, used, or new parts. You might also be able to find good buys in home-shopper guides or in the classified-advertisement section of your local newspaper.

Software (the programs that run on the computer) isn't cheap either. Computer games and information disks can cost $50 and up. A basic package of preloaded software is often the way to go, and there are numerous mail order companies that will custom-build your computer and software to meet your needs.

If you simply have no room in your budget for a new computer, don't give up. I've seen many donated computers in churches. Businesses often phase out computers every so often and are glad to give their "older" machines to churches for tax write-offs. Put your name in the hat with some of the larger businesses in your area and see what happens. You might also get a donation from an individual. It does happen!

bonus idea

If you're concerned about your teenagers improperly using the Internet, please be aware that there are ways to block certain words, phrases, or websites. One way is to have adult supervision. Another way is to check with your online carrier for details about blocking.

Having a computer in your youth area can be a plus, particularly if your teenagers spend free time in the area and might use it for homework or browsing on the World Wide Web. There are now hundreds of CD-ROM packages that contain information on everything from the Bible to church history to Christian music and video. Growing a library of such materials for younger teenagers might help you ride the wave of the future.

If you're looking at purchasing a computer for your youth room, you might do well to establish some guidelines and rules before beginning the process. People in church leadership may be skittish when it comes to computers. You might try to clear up some of the misconceptions and judgments about the Internet as you work toward your goal. Use examples that will demonstrate to church members how a computer will help your ministry to teenagers.

In the end, everyone will be a winner—especially the teenagers.

game

Computer Scavenger Hunt

THEMES: *the Internet, teamwork*

MATERIALS: *at least two computers with modems and connections to online service providers and lists of items to find on the Internet*

By now you've probably had your share of video scavenger hunts, instant-print camera scavenger hunts, Bible scavenger hunts, and every other type of seek-and-find game you can think of. But have you tried a computer scavenger hunt? Here's how to set one up.

You'll need at least two computers with online capabilities. Using home computers will work—you'll just have to work out the logistics of which team goes to which home.

Next, divide the group into teams (one team for each computer). Give each team a list of items they must find on the Internet, download and print, and bring to the starting point within the designated time. Some suggested items to find on the Internet are a professional sports team, the White House, a tennis shoe, a celebrity photo, an encyclopedia entry, a newspaper, a church web page, a song, a foreign website, a college web page, a photo of a giraffe, a movie review, and a Bible translation.

Once you've given each team a list of items, set a time limit, turn the teenagers loose, and wait for the first team to return. You might award points for each item based upon difficulty.

If you're computer illiterate, don't despair. Just find someone who knows the World Wide Web. There are plenty of computer users out there who would love to help you set up a computer scavenger hunt, provide help with "surfing" the World Wide Web, and give your group specific, detailed instructions.

E-MAIL ADDRESS

COST: *$0-$10 per month*
WORK LEVEL: *easy*
TIME INVOLVED: *short-term*
MATERIALS: *software from any online service and a computer with a modem*

If you have a computer, you might want to take advantage of online capabilities and e-mail features. Since teenagers are increasingly plugging into the World Wide Web, many of them can be reached through their Internet connections.

bonus idea

Train your e-mail ministry team to record the e-mail addresses of friends. Keep a list of these e-mail addresses. In the future, you may find that you'll utilize these addresses far more than traditional mailing addresses. E-mail will certainly become the communication preference for many teenagers in the years ahead.

Establishing an e-mail account is easy. All you have to do is load software from any online service provider. Choose a screen name for your account, and you can begin receiving e-mail right away. Most online services cost less than $10 a month, and the software can be obtained from any online service provider. Some companies actually provide e-mail service (without Internet access) for free.

Having an e-mail account for the youth group can have some definite advantages. Teenagers will be able to correspond with youth leaders and each other, and you can save money on postage and other materials by sending letters, reminders, and messages over the line to teenagers who have their own e-mail accounts.

Once you've established your e-mail account, I'm certain you'll find many creative ways to use it.

service project
E-mail Pals

THEMES: *the Internet, service, sharing faith*
MATERIALS: *a computer connected to an online service*

Now that teenagers are used to using the Internet and e-mail features on computers, invitational evangelism has never been easier.

If you'd like to create a ministry opportunity for the teenagers in your group, why not form an e-mail ministry team? It's easy.

Interested teenagers can invite their friends to youth group events by sending e-mail letters. You might help by drafting a few invitations the teenagers can use. Make these letters short, humorous, and above all, sincere. Each teenager can then personalize the e-mail letters before sending them to friends.

Using e-mail this way is less threatening for most teenagers than making or receiving a phone call. Through the use of computers, other teenagers can be invited to your group, your teenagers can learn how to invite others, and your youth group may grow.

WEBSITE

COST: *$50-$100*
WORK LEVEL: *easy*
TIME INVOLVED: *short-term*
MATERIALS: *a web-page design program for your computer*

A website on the World Wide Web is much different from an e-mail account. Having a website for your youth group puts you on the World Wide Web of information, which many people "surf," and can provide the teenagers in your youth group with more information than a regular account with an online service provider.

For example, a website can include pictures of your youth group, graphics, photos, abundant text, and an ever-changing portfolio of group events. The site can add color, depth, and variety to your services and ministries to teenagers.

Now, thanks to a host of new software options, creating your own website has never been easier. Prior to the advent of these software packages, putting a website on the World Wide Web meant learning a complicated set of codes. But innovative software programs have now simplified the process immensely.

Some of the best web-page design programs on the market can be found for less than $50. Most of these integrate into the word processing features of your computer, automatically converting documents into the right language. Other web-page makers allow you to include images and colors. You can find these programs in computer stores or retail outlets that carry software. Instead of buying a design program, you may be able to find free programs on the Internet (known as shareware) to help you set up your website.

If you're wanting to create a website for your youth group, consider that a website can keep your teenagers abreast of the latest events and times of upcoming outings. Teenagers will be attracted to the photos and images you can create—even photos of the teenagers themselves. You can use the website as a supplement to your newsletter. And unlike paper, a website "cleans up" easily, and you can change the format with the mere stroke of a key.

If you want to check out some of the church websites and youth ministry websites already on the Internet, simply ask someone who "surfs" frequently to show you how to find them. There are hundreds to see, and they can give you some great ideas.

 discussion starter

Web Surfing

THEMES: *the Church, technology*
MATERIALS: *a computer with access to the Internet*

For a quick discussion starter, pull up a church website on the computer. Gather your youth group around the monitor, and allow everyone an opportunity to peruse the information. Then ask:

● What is your impression of this particular congregation?

● What activities of this church look appealing to you, and why?

● If we were going to highlight our youth ministry on the World Wide Web, what ministries and events would be important for us to include?

● What words would best describe our youth group?

bonus idea

Make a list of the teenagers' best responses, and use these ideas to plan your website. You might consider adding graphics, text, and subheadings.

● What should be the relationship between the church and expanding technology?

Once kids have answered these questions and finished their discussion, set up an opportunity for the teenagers to compose their own website. Bring in some computer "experts" to help with this task as needed (but you'll be amazed at how many teenagers already know how to do it)!

VIDEO CAMERA

COST: *$400-$500*
WORK LEVEL: *easy*
TIME INVOLVED: *long-term*
MATERIALS: *a video camera and a videotape*

Like computers, video cameras continue to go down in price as the quality improves. A good video camera can now be purchased for less than $500. Many youth groups and churches make use of video cameras on a weekly basis.

I'm aware of one church that uses a video camera to tape special events in the life of the congregation. The videotapes become part of the historical records of the church. This congregation believes that years from now, people will want to view their entire spiritual history—the highlights of their faith—including baptisms and dedications, children's pageants, family gatherings, class outings, and worship services. Instead of looking up dusty records of paper and ink, people will be able to actually watch history unfold.

This concept is a fascinating one, and it might have some wonderful relevance for youth ministry. Perhaps we don't do enough with video. Teenagers love to watch television and movies. What better way to make them feel a part of things than by videotaping the special moments in your youth group—Super Bowl parties, service projects, mission trips, meaningful lessons, fun outings, lock-ins, and graduations? The impact can be great.

A Year to Remember

THEMES: *fellowship, giving*

MATERIALS: *videotapes, a video camera, a Bible*

Once you have your video camera, try making a yearlong video titled "A Year to Remember." Every time you have a significant youth event, plan to videotape a portion of it (a parent volunteer may be able to run the video camera). When you've finished your video, edit it. You could hire a professional video-editing service to dub in sound and special effects (usually for less than $50).

Once you have your master tape, gather the youth group for a special end-of-the-year party to watch the retrospective. No doubt you'll have plenty of laughs, a few tears, and a wealth of wonderful memories.

You might also add a bit of learning to your end-of-the-year party by reading Hebrews 12:1-2 and asking a few of these questions:

● How has our youth group become a part of that gathering of witnesses?

● Who are some of the witnesses we have known?

● How have these witnesses influenced our lives?

● What signs of God's love have we seen in each other this past year?

● What do you hope we can repeat next year?

● What was your most profound experience with God this past year?

● What did you enjoy the most?

● Whom will you miss?

bonus idea

Make copies of the videotape for everyone in the youth group, or if you prefer, give copies away as graduation gifts for your high school seniors. A videotape of this nature would be a cherished keepsake. And if you do this year after year, you could compile an entire high school chronology for your graduating young people. This would be a gift of faith and love which might help sustain them through the lonely times of college or job transition and the challenges of early adulthood.

ideas: multimedia

CD PLAYER

COST: *$150-$200*
WORK LEVEL: *easy*
TIME INVOLVED: *short-term*
MATERIALS: *a CD player and CDs*

When youth leaders ask how they can spice up their youth meetings, there is one sure solution—music.

Far too often, when I visit youth groups in other churches, there is no music at all. Furthermore, most youth rooms I've seen have little in the way of sound systems for music. Having a strong music ministry in place is vital. Teenagers are attracted to music. Teenagers also learn from music, find community through it, and surround themselves with it. If the church fails to provide attractive music for its young people, it's missing a golden opportunity to speak to teenagers "where they live."

Fortunately, a good sound system doesn't have to cost a pile of money. Portable CD players can be purchased for less than $200. A quality system with wall speakers can be purchased for around $500. Either way, it's a wise investment for the youth group.

CD players have become the standard in the music industry, and most teenagers seem to prefer high-quality CDs to cassette tapes. Furthermore, all musical styles, including contemporary Christian music, are now manufactured with CDs in mind.

Having a CD player on hand can add so much to any youth ministry. With a little help from your teenagers, you should be able to provide songs that will be uplifting as well as wholesome. You can use music to begin your meetings or to welcome teenagers as they enter the room. A CD player can also be used for worship times, sing-alongs, learning opportunities, and dances.

worship idea

Make a Joyful Sound

THEMES: *music, praise, worship*
MATERIALS: *pens or pencils, paper, CDs, a CD player, a chalkboard and chalk or newsprint and markers, and a Bible*

Prepare for this worship experience by working with a couple of your teenagers ahead of your scheduled meeting time. Listen to a wide range of contemporary Christian music, and pick out a half-dozen songs which have uplifting lyrics and beat and focus on adoration of God. Make note of these songs, the artists, and where to find them.

At the beginning of the youth meeting, have everyone sit in a circle. Give each person a pencil or pen and paper and then read aloud Psalm 98.

Say: **Today as we worship God, let us adore God through song. As we play each song, jot down some of your feelings about God as you experience the words and the music.**

bonus idea

Vote on a theme song from among the CD selections to serve as your group song. Use this song at special events and worship times.

Play your selected songs and then invite teenagers to respond to these questions:

● **In what ways did these songs make you feel closer to God?**

● **How would you describe your feelings toward God right now?**

● **What wonderful things has God done for you this week?**

Make a list of responses on a chalkboard or newsprint. Ask the teenagers to think about these responses before they leave the youth meeting.

As you close this worship experience, make a list of people the teenagers would like to pray for. Invite teenagers to offer prayers for these friends, acquaintances, and special needs. End the worship time with another song of praise.

BIG-SCREEN TELEVISION

COST: *$500-$1000*
WORK LEVEL: *easy*
TIME INVOLVED: *instant*
MATERIALS: *a big-screen television*

If you've ever had a Super Bowl party, you know how wonderful a big-screen television can be. And a big-screen television is great for showing videos and television programs.

A big-screen television may be used by many groups in the church—not just teenagers. For example, a summer day-camp can use it to show a daily movie. A women's group can watch the morning news while working on crafts. An aerobics class might use it for instruction and encouragement. Some churches may want to use televisions to run creative worship-videos during Sunday morning worship.

bonus idea

If you want your television to be mobile, a nice cart with large wheels and brakes can be found in most retail stores that carry bigger televisions. These carts range from $75 to $150.

Big-screen televisions come in many dimensions and styles. The televisions with the largest tubes (which have the clearest pictures) can be found for less than $500. Projection-screen televisions begin around $1000 and move upward in price as the screens and features grow larger and more sophisticated.

If you're planning to buy a television for your youth group or for other groups in your church, consider this rule of thumb before making your purchase: The size of the television screen will approximate the number of people who can comfortably watch it multiplied by two. For example, a twenty-inch television can be seen comfortably by forty people. A thirty-inch television can be seen by sixty.

As never before, teenagers are influenced by the power of images and television programming. Many youth ministries are taking advantage of the video age and are using televisions for worship, learning, and music. Furthermore, most Christian bookstores now carry a line of videos. Youth ministry videos have never been more accessible.

If you have some reservations about using television in your youth ministry, consider the fact that you can control what your teenagers are watching and you'll have their complete attention. Television can never be a substitute for human interaction, but showing an occasional movie clip, Christian video, or home video can add a new dimension to your teaching and keep your teenagers eager for more.

TV or Not TV

THEMES: *family, priorities, technology, television*

MATERIALS: *a television, a remote control, and costumes and props (optional)*

Here's a good skit to perform before showing your next video at a youth meeting. (See script on p. 88.) Teenagers can act out this skit, "TV or Not TV," as an opener. You'll need four actors. The rest of the group will participate by clapping for the characters with whom they most identify. For example, if some people identify most with Shondra, they should clap after she speaks her lines. Those who identify with Blake, Mom, or Dad should clap accordingly after their lines.

After the skit, ask the teenagers:

- What issues were being raised in this skit?
- Why did you identify with a certain character?
- What role should television play in our lives?
- What lessons have you learned from television programs?
- What suggestions do you have for this make-believe family?

Allow teenagers enough time to discuss these issues honestly and then lead into your video presentation with prayer.

MUSIC RACK

COST: *$25-$100*
WORK LEVEL: *easy*
TIME INVOLVED: *instant*
MATERIALS: *a rack for CDs or cassette tapes*

In addition to providing books (p. 61) or magazines (p. 73) for the youth group, you might also consider offering a collection of contemporary Christian CDs. Consider providing these on a checkout basis or allowing teenagers to purchase them.

Display your music collection on a CD or cassette-tape rack. These are inexpensive, and most racks will hold fifty or more selections.

One way to stock your music rack is to invite your teenagers to contribute CDs to the collection. Or you might find that joining

TV or Not TV

Characters

Blake (a teenager)
Shondra (the younger sister)
Mom
Dad

Script

(Shondra sits watching the television, munching on a bowl of popcorn, when Blake enters the room and grabs the remote control, changing the channel.)

Shondra: Hey, I was watching that show! Give me the remote control!

Blake: You've been hogging the set for hours. Now it's my turn. *Gilligan's Island* will be on in five minutes, and I want to find out if the professor can get a date with Mary Ann.

Shondra: Give me that remote!

Blake: No way.

Shondra: Mom! Dad! Blake is bugging me!

Mom: *(Enters with Dad)* What's going on here?

Shondra: I was watching a show, and Blake cut in and changed the channel.

Dad: Can't you two get along for even a minute?

Blake: Hey, no problem here. Talk to her. *(Points to Shondra.)*

Mom: Look, we're going to have to establish a few rules around here if we can't watch something together. Maybe we won't have TV in this house for a while.

Dad: Now, honey, let's not overreact. I want to watch the football game on Sunday.

Mom: *(Gives Dad "that look.")*

Shondra: I think we should have more than one TV.

Blake: I can spend more time at Jim's house. They've got a big-screen TV. It's great.

Mom: Why can't we just spend more time together as a family?

Dad: Aw, honey—let 'em watch their shows. What's the harm?

Blake: Yeah! What's wrong with Gilligan?

Shondra: I want to watch *The Little Princess Meets Dracula!*

Mom: Now that's gross.

Dad: Might be educational.

Blake: Might be stupid!

Mom: Television! Television! Television! I don't know what to do.

The whole family together: Somebody help us!

a Christian-music club would be a fast way to build a collection of top-notch selections.

If music has a central place in your youth ministry, consider all the fun you could have with a small library of good CDs or cassette tapes.

worship idea

Celebrations of Faith

THEMES: *celebration, joy, thankfulness*
MATERIALS: *a selection of contemporary Christian CDs or cassette tapes, a Bible, and a CD or cassette player*

Have teenagers form four groups. Invite each group to choose a favorite worship song from among the CDs or cassettes. If you have a very large group, you might want to have kids form more than four groups.

Have a volunteer read Colossians 3:15-17 aloud. Ask:

● Can you think of specific times when you've been thankful to God? How have you shown your thankfulness?

● Can you think of specific times when songs have lifted your spirits or inspired you? What happened?

● What do you think it means to sing "spiritual songs"?

Have kids form a prayer circle, and invite each teenager to offer a brief sentence prayer, completing this sentence: "Dear God, I'm thankful for..." If time allows, include a time of personal sharing as well so teenagers can express their needs to the rest of the group and ask for prayer. Others might wish to respond by offering a kind word.

After the time of prayer, have kids remain in the circle and play the selections of music the groups picked out at the beginning of the worship experience. Encourage teenagers to sing along with the music. You may want to allow them to accompany the songs with musical instruments (p. 156).

Close your worship time by reading Psalm 146 aloud.

bonus idea

After your worship time, you might want to use the CDs or cassette tapes for a dance or a sing-along party. Use the lyric sheets included in the cassette or CD cases to choose songs pertaining to a certain theme or biblical passage.

KARAOKE MACHINE

COST: *$200-$400*
WORK LEVEL: *easy*
TIME INVOLVED: *short-term*
MATERIALS: *a karaoke machine*

Karaoke machines have become quite popular in some corners of youth ministry. These machines usually cost less than $400 and can be great fun. A karaoke machine can also be used to teach new songs to your youth group and can give some of your talented singers a chance to lead your group in rousing sing-alongs.

Some of the better karaoke machines feature multiple microphones, recording and playback options, and other fun extras. With a bit of imagination, you should be able to get many useful and hilarious hours out of a karaoke machine. Over time, you might find it to be one of your most helpful youth ministry tools...and one of the tools most often requested by the kids.

Check out the karaoke machines in some of the larger electronics stores. Ask the salesperson to give you a demonstration and then crank up the volume and belt out a few bars.

One option for making a karaoke machine affordable might be to work with another youth group or organization to share in the cost, use, and ownership of the machine.

Once you have the machine in your youth room, try browsing through a selection of music at the local Christian bookstore. Most of the more popular contemporary Christian songs are available on cassette tapes that have been recorded specifically for voice-overs. Use these, along with lyrics sheets, to give your teenagers a taste of what it feels and sounds like to sing a big time hit. You may also want to ask your Christian bookstore about the availability of specifically Christian karaoke music.

bonus idea

A karaoke machine can also be a wonderful addition to worship times. You may have several teenagers in your group who would love to offer their singing talent to God. Not long ago I was blessed to have several teenagers (boys and girls) who offered to sing songs during our devotional times, at retreats, or at the closing of youth meetings. Never underestimate the impact your teenagers can have on one another—especially through a ministry of music. A karaoke machine is such a small thing, but it can reap big dividends!

Top o' the Charts

THEMES: *none*

MATERIALS: *a karaoke machine and a selection of contemporary Christian voice-over tapes or Christian karaoke tracks*

Have teenagers form groups of three or four. Invite each group to choose a song from among the selection of tapes that they, of course, will perform for the rest of the group. Give each group its own space and several minutes to decide who will sing each part of the song, if they'll sing the song straight or funny, and whether they'll use choreography.

Bring the groups together, and have them draw straws to see which group will go first. Encourage each group by clapping, singing along when invited to do so, and making the most of the fun. Invite teenagers to turn on the neon sign (p. 120) or use the strobe light (p. 165) if they want to. This is certain to be a repeat event if your teenagers get into the music.

Be prepared to have some extra funds on hand to buy additional songs for your machine—you're gonna need them!

ideas: multimedia

Creative Furnishings

DECORATIVE TELEPHONE

COST: *$25-$100*
WORK LEVEL: *moderate*
TIME INVOLVED: *short-term*
MATERIALS: *a decorative telephone*

Few things are more boring in a youth room than a drab, rotary-dial telephone with fingerprint patterns covering the handset. If you have such a phone in your youth area, why not trade it in for a new, decorative model? Perhaps you could find a pastel blue candlestick phone with a gold cradle or a phone shaped like a football. How about a mint-green phone with large buttons that glow in the dark or a phone shaped like a soccer ball?

Most of the telephones I've described can be purchased for less than $50, some for under $25. A unique telephone can give your youth room an aura of prestige or the feel of a playing field, or you can pick out a phone to complement the color of your decor.

If having a telephone attached to the wall is a problem, you can always go the cordless route. These phones run a bit higher in price, but they're still well under $100. You could keep the cordless phone in a closet, cabinet, or another locked area when it's not in use.

One sure way to get your teenagers involved is to bring in several styles of telephones and let your students make the final decision.

Cross-Country Calling

THEMES: *the body of Christ, friendship, unity*

MATERIALS: *Yellow Pages from other major cities, a time zone chart (sometimes in the telephone book itself), a telephone, a list of questions your youth group would like to ask a youth group in another city, and a bit of money for long-distance phone calls*

Here's a fun telephone outreach project you can do during a youth meeting. Not only is this game unpredictable and exciting, it also can be educational.

You'll need several phone books from large metropolitan areas around the country (most public and university libraries carry these). You'll also need a telephone. If possible, use a telephone with a speaker so the entire youth group can participate and listen in.

Look through the phone books of other cities, and pick out a few churches. Contact the churches before this activity to find out when and where their youth meetings are and to prepare youth groups for your calls. Check the time zone chart to make certain you'll be calling during youth meetings. In other words, you'll want to talk to other youth groups live!

bonus idea

After making your calls, take a few minutes to discuss what your teenagers learned about the church and about other youth groups. Ask questions like these:

● **How did this game help you understand the Christian faith?**

● **What new ideas did you receive from this adventure?**

Make a call and, using a list of prepared questions your group has put together beforehand, begin a conversation with members of the other youth group. This is a fun way to find out what other groups across the country are doing. You can learn about some of their most successful events, get a few new ideas, and swap faith stories. It's also an educational adventure, since your students will discover that teenagers are much the same all across the country and that there are many other Christian young people out there. If you use a speaker phone, everyone has an opportunity to participate and share in the laughter and questions. You might also wish to exchange names and addresses if you have the time. Your students might find a few pen pals in other states.

Close the game with a song or with prayer for the other youth groups you talked to.

ideas: creative furnishings

PATIO FURNITURE

COST: *$0-$200*
WORK LEVEL: *easy*
TIME INVOLVED: *instant*
MATERIALS: *patio furniture or folding lawn chairs*

E ver get the winter blahs? Ever wish you could have a bit of spring in the midst of the snow and ice? Well, unless you're lucky enough to live in a southern region, you know that winters can zap the life out of a youth group if teenagers have to stay cooped up for months. But there is hope.

Why not try some patio furniture as a way of curing the winter doldrums? A basic patio set can be found for less than $200 and might be just the thing to add new zest to your meetings. A patio set with a table and chairs can also be used as a snack bar, a study area, or a small-group discussion area.

If you're looking to use the patio set during the winter only, chances are you can find someone in your congregation who would be glad to lend you one. Most patio sets gather dust during the winter months. You could use the furniture and then return it before spring. Or should you be blessed with warm weather year-round, you could use the patio set for an outdoor youth-meeting every once in a while. Also, don't forget to check out garage sales if you want to pick up some inexpensive patio furniture you can use all year.

You could also use folding lawn chairs. Most aluminum-frame chairs with plastic webbing can be found for less than $15 and can be taken to retreats, campouts, and lock-ins. Folding chairs of this type have the advantage of taking up little space and being versatile. With a bit of creativity, you should be able to create a warm-weather mood.

game

Wandering in the Wilderness

THEMES: *the Exodus, Moses*
MATERIALS: *a folding lawn chair for each person, soft background music, and a Bible*

ere's a lawn-chair game that can double as an object lesson. You'll need a folding lawn chair for each student, soft background music (from *The Ten Commandments* if you have it), and a Bible. This game is similar to Musical Chairs—teenagers will walk around a row of lawn chairs (minus one), but instead of taking a seat when the music stops, they'll take a seat when a leader quits reading from the Bible.

To begin the game, say: **God's people have always been on the move. The ancient Israelites even wandered in the wilderness for forty years. Everything they owned was portable—including the tabernacle where they worshiped. Today we'll hear about all the places where the Israelites journeyed. As I begin reading from the Bible** (Numbers 33), **begin walking around the chairs. When I stop, you must shout out the name "Moses" and then find a seat. Whoever doesn't find a seat will become a settler in the Promised Land.**

Begin the game by reading slowly from Numbers 33. Every few moments, stop reading. Whoever doesn't find a seat is out of the game. Remove a chair, and continue reading and pausing until only one person remains. Then say: **Now everyone is settled in the Promised Land.**

Read the fulfillment of the Israelite journey, as found in Joshua 4.

bonus idea

Since many teenagers will connect Moses with the Ten Command-ments, use this as an opportunity to review the commandments. See if the group can work together to name all ten commandments (Exodus 20:1-17). Make the Ten Command-ments into a "top ten" list, print it up, and see if the teenagers can memorize them in this format.

BEACH UMBRELLA

COST: *$40-$50*
WORK LEVEL: *easy*
TIME INVOLVED: *instant*
MATERIALS: *a beach umbrella, beach blankets, a wading pool, sand, and videotapes and games (optional)*

If you're trying to cure the winter blahs and want to go a step further than the patio furniture (p. 94), you can go all the way to the beach. Bring in two or three children's wading pools, fill them with clean white sand (available in fifty-pound bags), set up a beach umbrella and a few blankets, and presto! You've created your very own beach party.

group builder

Beach Party

THEMES: *none*

MATERIALS: *snacks, games, blankets, music, children's wading pools, a beach umbrella, and sand*

Organizing a winter beach-party is more fun as a group project. Make sure every teenager in the group is assigned to bring something to add to the festivities: a snack, a game, sand, a blanket, music, or a videotape. You may want to assign some students to clean up or to lead devotions. Some might sing songs or play instruments.

A winter beach-party can be a wonderful group-builder. You can play beach games, eat snacks, and maybe have a barbecue. Do the limbo, dance, sing, and invite parents to participate. Watch a videotape of a '50s beach movie, laugh all evening, make sand castles, and go home with sand in your shoes!

bonus idea

Make your beach party a community event. Invite other youth groups to participate. Have your students announce the party at school. Arrange for a group of adults to bring in a grill and fix hot snacks.

After the party, send a thank you note to everyone who participated, or call visiting students to invite them to attend next week's youth meeting.

CEILING PARACHUTE

COST: *$100-$500*
WORK LEVEL: *moderate*
TIME INVOLVED: *short-term*
MATERIALS: *a parachute and supplies to attach it to the ceiling*

A parachute can serve as a lively game-option in warm weather and can double as a ceiling drape in the winter. And a colorful parachute can give a youth room a wonderful atmosphere of friendship and warmth.

Be sure to measure the dimensions of your room before purchasing a chute. They do come in various sizes, and they range in price from $100 to $500 or more.

If you plan to buy a parachute, school-sports catalogs often carry the widest selection. Check with a high school coach or athletic director. He or she should have several catalogs on hand. And if you're in the buying mood but you're on a fixed budget, you can find used chutes at army-surplus stores—although military chutes come in drab hues. With a little creativity, though, you can let your students paint some color onto a military parachute.

A properly anchored parachute can also serve as a decent storage area for lightweight sports items such as balls, nets, and rackets. Just secure the chute to the ceiling, and toss your items over the top.

If you want to surprise your students, ask your church trustees or custodians to help you hang the parachute. A good carpenter or custodian can hang the chute safely (usually by attaching eye screws into the ceiling and securing four corners of the chute with rope).

discussion starter

Leap of Faith

THEMES: *faith, spiritual heritage*

MATERIALS: *a parachute (hanging from the ceiling) and a Bible*

Have kids gather underneath the ceiling parachute, and invite everyone to lie down on the floor and look up at the parachute. Ask:

bonus idea

If you want to continue the discussion and talk about sharing faith, ask groups of teenagers to discuss these questions:

● How would you go about trying to convince someone else to trust in God?

● What would you give another person as a sign of God's security and faithfulness to help that person remember that God will never let him or her down?

● Has anyone here ever gone sky diving? (If so, allow teenagers to briefly describe their experiences.)

● What do you think sky diving would feel like?

● What are the risks involved in sky diving?

● What type of trust is involved in sky diving?

● As you look up at this parachute, do you think you would trust it to get you safely back to earth? Why or why not?

● How does hearing other people's stories affect your desire (or lack of desire) to go sky diving?

Read Hebrews 11:1 aloud. Ask:

● In what ways are trust and faith synonymous?

● How is trusting in God similar to jumping out of an airplane with a parachute? How is it different?

Ask volunteers to read aloud Hebrews 11:2-31, with each person reading one verse at a time. Ask:

● How does reading about other people's faith stories affect your willingness to put your faith in God?

BEANBAG CHAIRS

COST: *$0-$30 per chair*
WORK LEVEL: *easy*
TIME INVOLVED: *instant*
MATERIALS: *beanbag chairs*

One unique facet of youth ministry is that you don't have to have fancy furnishings or comfortable chairs. Kids can be right at home sitting on tables, on stools, or even on the floor. I've seen many youth rooms that take advantage of this fact and simply pile beanbag chairs along the wall.

Beanbag chairs are great for youth ministry because they're portable, versatile, and inexpensive. Most beanbag chairs cost less than $30 and are available in a variety of sizes and shapes. You can use them for games, parties, or overnighters, and once they grow flat, you can fill them with new stuffing to make them good as new.

I know of one youth group with personalized beanbags. The teenagers had purchased their own beanbag chairs and written their names on them.

Another group formed a Bible study area using beanbag chairs, floor mats, and magazine racks.

game
Beanbag Tick-Tack-Toe

THEMES: *none*
MATERIALS: *masking tape and eight beanbag chairs*

Here's a version of Tick-Tack-Toe that will get your kids in the mood for some serious fun. You'll need ten beanbag chairs (five marked with X's and five marked with O's). You'll also need to use masking tape to mark a giant Tick-Tack-Toe grid on the floor.

Have nine volunteers sit on the floor in the giant Tick-Tack-Toe

If you're short on funds for new beanbag chairs, initiate a churchwide effort. Call it "Adopt a Beanbag." People can sponsor beanbag chairs for the youth group by donating money. Those who participate can later be recognized in a youth meeting (perhaps by being the first ones to toss beanbags in a game of Beanbag Tick-Tack-Toe).

grid (one person in each space on the grid). Have the rest of the teenagers form two teams. Teams will take turns "tossing" the beanbag chairs to the people in the grid as they play a game of Tick-Tack-Toe. The young people on each team can alternate turns so each person has a chance to toss a bean-bag chair in an effort to get three in a row.

If you have a very large group, you may want to play more than one game at a time.

After playing the game a few times, try some of these variations to make the game more difficult, more fun, or more challenging:

- Blindfold the "tossers."
- Instruct the people inside the grid to use their hands, arms, and legs to deflect the beanbags.
- Blindfold the teenagers inside the grid.
- Instruct the tossers to toss the beanbags through their legs or over their heads.
- Rig up a giant slingshot made of huge rubber bands, and have players try catapulting the beanbags into the grid.

RADICAL FLOORS

COST: *$0-$50*
WORK LEVEL: *easy*
TIME INVOLVED: *short-term*
MATERIALS: *rugs, matting, paint, or another decorative floor covering*

Take a look at the floor in your youth room (if you have one). Is the carpet worn? Are the tiles chipped? Could it really use some color and vibrancy? New rugs might be the answer—or maybe some paint.

Over the years I've seen some radical floor-coverings in churches...everything from rummage sale rejects to handmade quilts. The idea is that floors don't have to be drab. They can be fun.

Here's a short list of some fantastic-floor ideas: Disney-character rugs, youth group footprints or hand prints painted on the floor, foreign rugs, mission-trip rugs, body outlines, floor signatures, rugs with areas marked for playing games, grass mats, beach blankets, doormats with slogans, a large round bull's-eye rug, rubber matting, plastic bread-wrapper rugs, and a Persian rug.

Your teenagers can collect all kinds of rugs or help create them. You should be able to find some rugs at rummage sales, or maybe people in your church will donate rugs or paint for you to use.

A good floor-covering can add much to an otherwise drab room. And rugs have the advantage of flexibility. You can change the look and color of the room without ripping up carpeting or repainting walls. If you choose to paint fun designs on the floor, you can always make use of rugs later.

affirmation

Body Outlines

THEMES: *love, self-esteem*
MATERIALS: *pencils, sidewalk chalk or paint and paintbrushes, music, and a Bible*

Have a volunteer read Genesis 1:26-31 aloud. Then say: **The story of Creation can remind us that we're all created in the image of God and each one of us is a unique creation of God. Today we're going to practice giving thanks for our uniqueness and affirm God's unique creation of each of us.**

While music is playing in the background, have kids form pairs. Invite each teenager to lie on the floor while his or her partner traces his or her body outline in pencil. When kids have traced each other's outlines, provide sidewalk chalk or paint and paintbrushes and instruct kids to trace over their pencil lines with the paint or chalk. When all the outlines are finished, allow some time for them to dry if teenagers used paint. Then invite each person to write an affirmation inside each other person's outline. Say: **Each of us has unique attributes, qualities, and talents that others recognize and admire. I'd like each of you to go to each of the other outlines and write inside the outline a word or phrase that describes something you admire about that person. For example, you might write "great smile," "good musician," "athletic,"**

Encourage your teenagers to lead this affirmation idea with children in a Sunday school class or another special setting. Teenagers love to teach smaller children, and kids of all ages really get into this affirmation.

or "caring." Go from body outline to body outline until you've written something for each person.

When everyone is finished writing, instruct group members to read and think about what others have written about them. Ask:

● What new things have you learned about each other from this experience?

● What do you think it means for you to be created in the image of God?

● How can we affirm each other more in our youth group?

Close by reading Psalm 139.

STUFFED ANIMALS

COST: *$0*
WORK LEVEL: *easy*
TIME INVOLVED: *instant*
MATERIALS: *a variety of stuffed animals*

I knew a young woman in college who had more than a hundred stuffed animals in her bedroom. Later, when she began directing a youth ministry at a nearby church, she took the stuffed animals to the youth room and sprinkled them everywhere. What she created was a wonderful, colorful atmosphere of caring and love.

If you want to do the same in your youth room, you could buy stuffed animals, but why would you want to? Every girl in your youth group probably has one or two she could part with. And even the guys might be willing to admit they have old teddy bears and other animals they would be glad to donate. Have your kids bring in their old stuffed animals, and make your youth room into a humane shelter for overloved toys. You'll be surprised at how these furry, fuzzy, and woolly creatures will transform your youth room overnight.

Another great thing about stuffed animals is that they can be removed quickly and easily. If you're meeting in a multipurpose room or a temporary space, you can store the stuffed animals in a box and take them out when you want to display or use them. Stuffed animals are one of the most versatile decorating ideas you'll find anywhere.

Furthermore, you can use these lovable creatures for games, devotions, object lessons, and worship times.

discussion starter

The Stuff We're Made Of

THEMES: *feelings, honesty, love*

MATERIALS: *stuffed animals (at least one per student) and a Bible*

Have kids form a circle, and dump a pile of stuffed animals in the middle (make sure there's at least one animal per person). Then say: Whenever we come to youth meetings, we bring our feelings—our hurts, pain, joy, sorrow, and worries. I'd like each of you to look through the pile and pick out a stuffed animal that reflects the way you're feeling today. You might pick an animal because of the color, the way it looks, the way it feels, or the way it is made. Be prepared to tell the rest of us why your stuffed animal reflects the way you're feeling today.

Allow time for the teenagers to look through the pile and choose stuffed animals. Then have each person in the circle share his or her feelings. Be prepared to encourage teenagers who are feeling down, lonely, afraid, sad, or hurt. If you think it's appropriate, you might try encouraging students with Bible verses such as Psalm 4:6-8, Proverbs 13:12, or Jeremiah 8:18. When everyone has had an opportunity to share, say: **Sometimes we don't realize that God created us with feelings. Feelings are important. And there are moments in our lives when we need to know that other people care about us. That's what our youth group is for. We can share our feelings with each other, and we can know that other people care about us.** Ask:

bonus idea

When you're finished with your stuffed animals or after they've served in the youth room for some time, use these lovable toys to reach out to others through a youth service project. Clean the stuffed animals and take them to nursing homes, children's homes, hospitals, or homeless shelters and give them away. Talk to the residents, and let them know they're not forgotten. The stuffed animals can be reminders of your Christian love.

- What makes you feel good when you attend youth meetings?
- What makes you feel bad when you attend youth meetings?
- Why do you think it's so difficult for some people to share feelings?
- How can we be more attentive to each other's feelings?
- How can this youth group help you feel more comfortable sharing your feelings?

Close the discussion starter with a group hug.

FOOTBALL FIELD

COST: *$0-$25*
WORK LEVEL: *difficult*
TIME INVOLVED: *long-term*
MATERIALS: *indoor-outdoor carpeting, paint, and paintbrushes*

Several years ago, I read a fascinating home-improvement article about a father who had fixed up his son's bedroom to look like a baseball field. The father had painted four bases on the floor, provided an infield and an outfield, and he had painted the walls to look like major-league fences and stands with screaming fans and popcorn salesmen.

It wasn't long after I read this article that I walked into a youth room in Tennessee and noticed that the teenagers there had undertaken a similar project. They had unrolled a strip of green indoor-outdoor carpeting and painted lines on it (with enamel paint) to make it look like a miniature football-field. Goal posts had been painted on the walls, and a model of the Goodyear Blimp hung from the ceiling. Since the carpet wasn't glued to the floor, the kids could roll it up when they wanted to have other activities in the same area—an advantage of this type of carpet.

When I talked with the youth leader, I learned that the group used the football field for a variety of games and crowdbreakers. The lines were used for all sorts of relay races.

At first glance, this type of project looks like an expensive undertaking. But in reality, a football field can be constructed for next to nothing. Consider first that green indoor-outdoor carpeting can usually be found on clearance at many carpet outlets. Also, many people would be glad to donate a strip of this carpeting. As for the walls, all you need are paints in several colors, a few brushes, and a game plan.

group builder

Fabulous Football

THEMES: *perseverance, sports, teamwork*

MATERIALS: *white enamel spray-paint, assorted colored paints, paintbrushes, masking tape, and a Bible*

Constructing a football field in your youth room can be a fun group project, especially during football season. Make it a party, and involve everyone!

Once you've found a piece of carpet, use masking tape to mark the lines of a football field on the carpet. (Don't worry about the number of lines unless you're a football perfectionist.) Draw a rough pencil-sketch of your grandstand and goal posts on the wall so you'll have a general idea of what you need to paint. (Be sure to enlist all your artistically talented teenagers to help with these details.)

Once you're ready to begin, make sure everyone has a job to do and be sure you have all the supplies you'll need to complete the project. Then

bonus idea

Plan to make your football field at the beginning of January so you can break in the new decor with a **Super Bowl party.**

turn your students loose!

Working on something of this magnitude makes for a good overnight project. You can complement your time together by having popcorn breaks, playing fun games, and laughing together.

COOL CURTAINS

COST: *$0-$100*
WORK LEVEL: *moderate*
TIME INVOLVED: *short-term*
MATERIALS: *curtains or fabric for curtains*

Early in my youth ministry, I inherited one of the ugliest youth rooms ever seen. In an effort to give the room a face lift, I threw away old furnishings, brought in new cabinets, and gave the place a new coat of paint. Still, I knew there was something missing. "What you need are new curtains," said an elderly lady who happened to peek in one day. "Curtains make the room."

She was right. I'm glad she suggested it. I had overlooked the fact that the curtains were as drab as dust—old strands of faded cloth that had been hanging for three decades. The next day I took them down and asked the same woman (an important trick of the trade) if she would help me pick out some new curtains. She was more than happy to volunteer!

In a few weeks she had sewn a new set of curtains for the youth room. They were fantastic—bright, sunny, breezy-looking curtains that picked up an otherwise drab room and transformed it into a homey space for teenagers.

I can't tell you what kind of curtains are right for your youth room, but I can tell you that draperies are expensive. If you need new curtains, I suggest that you find a volunteer to sew them for you. Professional window-treatments will be out of the price range for most youth budgets, but you can probably afford to buy the fabric or you might be able to find less expensive curtains at a discount store.

Once you have your curtains installed, you'll find that a set of vibrant curtains can transform a room, adding an important sense of warmth.

Insiders and Outsiders

THEMES: *acceptance, cliques, communication, racism*
MATERIALS: *paper, black markers, and a Bible*

Try using the windows in your youth room to teach a valuable lesson about cliques, racism, and the importance of communication. Be sure to use this devotion on a sunny, warm day.

You'll need to open the drapes and blinds of one window so people can see in and out. Then divide your group into two teams— Insiders, who will stay in the room, and Outsiders, who will go outside. Give each team several sheets of paper and a black marker.

Begin the devotion with these instructions: **Pretend for a moment that we live in a strange society where Outsiders and Insiders can't mingle. They never have, and they never will. Outsiders, though, have always wanted to be Insiders, but the Insiders have forbidden it. And Outsiders and Insiders can communicate with each other only through the written word. You can only speak to your own kind. These are the rules of our society. Now I'd like the Outsiders to go outside while the Insiders stay inside.**

Allow time for the Outsiders to go to the other side of the window. Stay inside, and begin the devotion with these instructions to the Insiders: **I'd like you to remember the rules of our society. But as you can see, the Outsiders want in, and they're waiting for a message. What message will you write?**

Give the Insiders time to write a message. Hold the paper up to the window so the Outsiders can read it and then close the curtains.

After a few moments, open the curtains and see if the Outsiders have responded with a message or a request of their own. If so, instruct the Insiders to write a reply, and again close the curtains. If the Outsiders fail to respond to the Insiders' message, encourage the Insiders to keep writing messages

bonus idea

Before teenagers leave, present them with this challenge for the coming week: "Go forth and break down walls between Insiders and Outsiders."

until the Outsiders respond. Continue to send messages back and forth until it's clear that the Insiders have reached a stalemate with the Outsiders or the Insiders allow the Outsiders to come in.

Have the Outsiders come back inside. Ask kids these questions:

- How did it feel to be an Outsider?
- How did it feel to be an Insider?
- What was difficult about this situation?
- Insiders, why did you decide not to allow (or to allow) the Outsiders to come in? How did you reach that decision?
- What aspects of our own society do you see represented in this game?
- Why do you think we often find it difficult to communicate with other people in our society? at school? at youth group? in the church?
- Who do you think are the Insiders in our society? Who are the Outsiders?
- How can Christians break down barriers between people?

Have kids re-form their two groups (Insiders and Outsiders) and read aloud Galatians 3:23-29 in their groups. Invite the two groups to write down their impressions of what this Scripture passage says about what they experienced. Have groups present their findings to each other and then ask:

- How do we need to change if we are to achieve the vision of this Scripture passage?

QUILTS

COST: *$0-$500*
WORK LEVEL: *easy*
TIME INVOLVED: *instant*
MATERIALS: *a quilt or quilt materials*

One evening my wife and I watched the movie *How to Make an American Quilt*. It's the story of some older women who are part of a quilting circle. In the movie they have come together to make a wedding quilt for a young woman who is having second thoughts about her fiancé. As I watched this movie, I realized that for many older women, quilting circles provided far more than a job. These quilting circles became families; circles of friendship where life was discussed in detail and joys and sorrows were shared and woven into a rich fabric, much like a story.

Over the years I've noticed more and more quilts hanging in youth rooms. Perhaps these quilts have been donated, made by groups within the church, or commissioned by the youth group. I do know that a quilt makes an excellent wall-hanging, and nearly every quilt has a story behind it.

If there is a quilting circle in your church, find out if the circle might be willing to make a quilt for the youth room. If so, you could probably provide the materials for less than $50. Or if you know someone who has quilted much over the years, you might ask to purchase a quilt (good ones usually sell for $500 or more) or to pay a smaller sum to hang it on the youth-room wall for a period of time. Many quilters consider themselves artists and are willing to have their work displayed in public places at no charge. See what you can work out.

A quilt might be just the thing you need to cover an ugly wall or to spice up a lackluster multipurpose room.

devotion

A Stitch in Time

THEMES: *faith, patience*

MATERIALS: *a needle and thread for each student, a scrap of cloth for each student, a quilt, paper, pencils, and Bibles*

Do you know someone in your church who quilts? Don't waste that talent. Invite the quilter to attend your youth group when you lead this devotion about patience. Either have the quilter bring a quilt to the meeting, or find a quilt that you can display for the group.

Display the quilt and then invite your guest to talk briefly about the art of quilting and how it is done. Then give each student a needle and some thread, and say: **Now that you know how a quilt is made, I'd like each of you to try your hand at making a stitch or two. Hold your piece of material and your needle and thread, and try to follow**

bonus idea

If you are a truly adventuresome youth leader, invite your special guest to lead your group in making a quilt. Make certain you have all the necessary materials. You may need to work on the quilt for at least several weeks to complete it.

our guest's instructions.

Allow your guest to lead the students step by step through the process of making several stitches. As teenagers work on this task, lend encouragement and assistance as necessary.

When kids are finished stitching, ask:

● How many of you think you would like to make a quilt?

● Do you think this art would be easy or difficult? Why?

Give each person a Bible, and ask a volunteer to read Hebrews 6:11-12 aloud. Then ask:

● Why is it often difficult for us to be patient?

● What kinds of things test your patience?

Give each person a pencil and paper. Ask each teenager to make a "top ten" list of things that test his or her patience. Let each teenager read his or her list for the rest of the class.

Invite group members to read 2 Peter 3:8-9 and then ask:

● What does this passage tell us about the nature of God's patience?

● In what ways does the quilt remind you of God's patience toward us?

● How can we be more patient with each other, modeling God's patience in our lives?

After discussion, gather around the quilt for prayer and a song.

POTTER'S WHEEL

COST: *$20-$350*
WORK LEVEL: *easy*
TIME INVOLVED: *short-term*
MATERIALS: *a potter's wheel, water, pottery paints (optional), aprons, clay, and plastic floor covering*

There may be times when you would like to emphasize a biblical theme in your youth room. The image of the potter's wheel is one used throughout the Scriptures (Isaiah 64:8; Jeremiah 18:1-6; 19:1-11; Lamentations 4:2; Romans 9:21; and Revelation 2:27). Many teenagers, though, have never seen a potter's wheel and would find one fascinating.

Check with your local art-supply dealer. Most art-supply stores have one or two wheels on hand, or they can order one for you. An electric potter's wheel costs around $300, but you can find manual or foot-powered wheels for $15 and up. Potter's clay is inexpensive and comes in a variety of textures. Speak with your art-supply dealer about the various types of wheels and clays, and he or she will be able to help you work something into your budget.

You may want to use the potter's wheel as a decorative piece in the youth room, or if you're adventuresome, you might attempt to fashion some clay pots or mugs. Without a kiln, however, you won't be able to harden the clay to its fullest, but you can still create some fine decorative pieces by allowing the clay creations to dry in the hot sun. They'll function as decorations, but don't try to get them to hold water!

You might also plan a Bible lesson around the potter's wheel, make decorative mugs for a fund-raiser, or use the wheel as an object lesson. If you're going to use the wheel, be sure to have plenty of aprons, a plastic covering for the floor, and an adequate supply of clay. You'll also need a water supply and some pottery paints.

 object lesson

Potter and Clay

THEMES: *grace, love*
MATERIALS: *potter's clay, a potter's wheel, and a Bible*

Use the potter's wheel in this object lesson to illustrate God's grace. Invite teenagers to gather around the potter's wheel. Give each person a lump of clay, and give these instructions: **I'd like you to fashion your own drinking cup with your hands. Make certain there are no imperfections in your design. After everyone is finished, we'll vote on the best cup.**

As teenagers are working on their cups, begin to spin the potter's wheel and work with a raw lump of clay, fashioning a jar as you tell this story:

Once there was an expert potter (pause). He loved to make things (pause). In fact, he made everything that exists (pause): the plants, trees, fish, and animals (pause); the bees and insects, the birds and flowers. But one day he said, "I'd like to make some people in my image" (pause). And so he made a man (pause). And then he made a woman (pause). And the potter looked at them and said, "It is good" (pause).

Every day the potter watched to see what the man and woman would do (pause). He noticed that they loved the other creatures he had fashioned (pause). They loved the birds and animals, the trees, and the flowers (pause). They loved each other (pause). But the man and woman did not love the potter (pause).

Even so, the potter was good to the man and woman (pause). He gave them food to eat, lovely places to go, and a wonderful world of beauty (pause). But still they did not love the potter (pause).

One day the potter looked at his creation and realized the man and woman had rebelled against his love. (Remove your clay jar from the potter's wheel.) Like clay jars, the man and woman needed to be mended (pause). Because they had rejected the love and care of the potter, they had become broken (pause) and shattered in places (pause). But still the potter loved what he had made (pause). He wanted to make his creation whole again (pause).

After the story, ask:

● Why do you think the potter loved his creation?

● Why do you think the man and woman rebelled against the potter's love?

● How do you think the potter would go about making the man and woman whole again?

bonus idea

As an optional closing, display the drinking cups the teenagers have fashioned and read Isaiah 64:8.

Read Ephesians 2:8-10 aloud. Ask:

● In what ways is God like a potter?

● How does God act toward us?

Now ask the teenagers to show you the drinking cups they have fashioned with their modeling clay. Ask:

● Was it easy or difficult for you to make your cup? Explain.

● Do you see imperfections in your creation? How do you feel about your creation?

- How good do we have to be for God to love us?
- What does God's grace mean to you?

Ask students to offer prayers for each other. Allow teenagers to take their cups home. Unless you fire them in a kiln, remind kids that their cups won't hold water.

GAS PUMP

COST: *$0-$500*
WORK LEVEL: *easy*
TIME INVOLVED: *short-term*
MATERIALS: *an antique gas pump*

One of the most unique youth rooms I have seen featured a fun spiritual theme. As teenagers entered the room they filed past an antique gas pump displaying the words "The Filling Station." The youth leader explained to me: "We think kids need a place for spiritual rejuvenation and renewed energy. And so we invite them to come to this place—this filling station—to find the friends and loving support they need during this period of adolescence."

When I asked where he found the antique gas pump, he told me they were available in antique shops, novelty stores, junkyards, and sometimes through gasoline companies. He was right. A few months later I came upon an antique gas pump at an antique mall. The price was a bit hefty, around $500, but the pump was in excellent condition and would have made a beautiful addition to any youth area.

Even if you can't find an antique gas pump, the next time you're in an antique shop, stroll around and see if you can spot a few unique items for the youth area. You'll be amazed at the ideas you'll find lurking on dusty shelves.

Gas-Pump Scavenger Hunt

THEMES: *cooperation, teamwork*

MATERIALS: *at least two video cameras, transportation, adult drivers, and lists of items found at gas stations*

Once you have an antique gas pump in your room, try using this team-building scavenger hunt to bring your kids closer together.

Before this activity, make a list of items that can be found at gas stations (such as air and water pumps, engine oil, advertisements, tires, air fresheners, and car washes). Assign points to each item, based on your assessment of how easy or difficult it will be for the teenagers to locate it. Make a photocopy of this list for each video camera you have.

Have kids form as many teams as you have video cameras. Give each group a video camera, a photocopy of the list of items to find, and a time limit. Assign each team to an adult driver. Instruct teams to find and videotape as many of the items on the list as possible within the time allowed. Say: **As you travel from filling station to filling station in search of these items, you must videotape each one with your entire group in the picture. Only those items videotaped with the entire group will receive points. And you must complete the hunt within the time limit. For each minute your team is late getting back, ten points will be deducted from your total score. Naturally, the object is to get as many points as possible.**

Make sure each group knows what time you'll be meeting. At the designated time, return to the meeting place and watch the videotapes—they'll be hilarious. Issue prizes to the winning team if you want to.

bonus idea

After watching the videotapes, spend some time considering the gas pump in your youth area. Work with the group to come up with a unique name or slogan for your room or your group. Try to capture the idea of being "filled," "fueled up," or "energized" for God.

BICYCLE RACK

COST: *$80-$200*
WORK LEVEL: *easy*
TIME INVOLVED: *instant*
MATERIALS: *a bicycle rack*

bonus idea

Invite the teenagers to help decide where to place the bicycle rack in the youth room. Try to make the rack accessible to the teenagers who bring bicycles and yet unobtrusive to others. Brainstorm a few ideas on how to accomplish this.

If you live in an area where bicycles are plentiful and teenagers are accustomed to riding to youth meetings, you might want to find a bicycle rack for the youth room. Larger racks—the type found at schools—can be ordered through athletic-department catalogs (see a high school coach or athletic director). These usually cost around $200. Smaller racks are available in bicycle shops and usually cost less than $80.

A bicycle rack may not be considered decor, but it can be practical if you have several bicyclists in the youth group. It can also serve to encourage young people to ride their bicycles, promoting great exercise, cleaner air, and less money spent on fuel.

skit

The Good Neighbor

THEMES: *compassion, hope, love, service*
MATERIALS: *bicycles, costumes (optional)*

bonus idea

After the skit, ask these questions:

● What parable of Jesus does this skit remind you of?

● How is this skit different from the parable?

● What lessons do the skit and the parable teach?

● What does it mean to love your neighbor as yourself?

Should you have a bicycle rack and several bicycles in the youth room, perform the quick skit on page 116 to get your kids thinking and talking about neighborly love.

The Good Neighbor

Characters:

Bicyclist (nerdy-looking man on a bicycle)
Athlete (serious athlete on a bicycle)
Woman (on a bicycle)
Teenager (on a bicycle, holding a loud portable stereo)
Motorcyclist (tough, scary-looking man on a motorcycle)

Script

Bicyclist: *(Rides his bike across the stage area, falls off his bike, and lies injured along the roadside. In agony, he clutches his ankle, looks around, and then decides to call out for help.)* Help! Somebody! I think I've broken my ankle!

Athlete: *(As he rides by, he pauses, but he refuses to stop.)* Sorry, buddy. I'm training for a triathlon. Can't stop now!

Bicyclist: Please wait! Come back! *(A few moments pass. He clutches his ankle in pain and then sees another approaching bicyclist.)* Hey! Help! I think I've broken my ankle!

Woman: *(Stops abruptly, but then quickly rides away.)* I'm sorry. I don't want to get involved. I'm sorry.

Bicyclist: No! Please come back! I won't hurt you! I can't even walk! *(Another long moment of agony passes. Finally he sees another bicyclist approaching.)* Hey! Please stop!

Teenager: *(Rides by, holding a blaring portable stereo. Stops, peers down at the man, and smiles.)* Hey, dude! Whoa! That's a nasty ankle you got there!

Bicyclist: *(Shouting over the loud music.)* Thank heavens you stopped! I think my ankle is broken.

Teenager: Cocaine? Oh man, I've done that gig before. Nasty stuff. You ought to try Jesus. Hang in there, dude. *(Waves as he rides off, listening to the loud music.)*

Bicyclist: No, not cocaine! Broken! (Sees an approaching motorcyclist.) Help! Someone! Anyone!

Motorcyclist: *(Rides by, making loud "revving" noises. Stops and gets off his "motorcycle.")* What's up, pop?

Bicyclist: Oh, thank goodness. Go get help. I think I've broken my ankle.

Motorcyclist: Hang in there, daddy. I'll be right back with help. *(Hops on his motorcycle and begins to ride away.)*

Bicyclist: *(Calls out to the motorcyclist as he begins to leave.)* Wait! Why did you stop? Tell me why you stopped.

Motorcyclist: *(Stops and smiles.)* I learned about this kind of stuff in Sunday school and youth meetings. What else?

OVERHEAD PROJECTOR

COST: *$0-$200*
WORK LEVEL: *easy*
TIME INVOLVED: *instant*
MATERIALS: *an overhead projector and transparencies*

O verhead projectors have been around for years, and many churches have projectors that are gathering dust in closets. The problem is, most overhead projector presentations are dull and boring. People tire of the endless flipping of transparencies and the lecture-style format. But an overhead projector can be a great asset in a youth area—if utilized well.

For example, try using an overhead projector to present images or Bible verses to enhance a worship service. You can also use the overhead projector to display song lyrics (once you get permission from the publishers), to present instructions for games such as scavenger hunts, to show off your own animated characters to help illustrate your next lesson, or to reinforce active-learning activities with pithy concepts and slogans that will help teenagers remember important ideas.

Overhead projectors can be purchased through office-supply catalogs and in large stores that cater to business people. An average unit costs about $150-$200. But chances are, you can find a used projector from another church. (I recently saw two in a church rummage sale.) You might also check the supply closets in your own facility—it's amazing how many churches have them but don't know it.

If you use an overhead projector sparingly or as an addition to your active-learning lessons, teenagers will often latch onto an image or an idea if it's presented properly. I know that many teenagers do learn from reading, and a key concept here and there can be projected as an aid to remembering.

When I was a teenager, I had a poster in my bedroom—a beautiful mountain scene with a waterfall spilling over dark and dangerous-looking rocks. I had this poster hanging on the inside of my closet door, so every time I opened the door, I read these words: "Do not pray for an easy life...pray to be a strong person." I've never forgotten those words, because the image flashes constantly across my mind and the poster used only a few words to

ideas: creative furnishings

convey a dense message.

If you use an overhead projector in this manner—to convey a message in few words and to display powerful images—teenagers will remember, especially if the message is reinforced from time to time.

Some youth groups have statements of purpose or focus for the year. Use the overhead projector to keep these larger aims before your group each week. Remind. Remind. Remind. Choose your moments to blend a powerful worship experience or a devotion with these reminders.

worship idea

For God So Loved...

THEMES: *grace, love*
MATERIALS: *an overhead projector, overhead transparencies, and newspapers*

Use your overhead projector as part of this wonderful worship experience.

As you begin the worship time, project the words of John 3:16 onto the wall on an overhead transparency. Invite three teenagers to read this verse aloud, with the first one emphasizing the word "God," the second person emphasizing the word "loved," and the third emphasizing the word "world."

Invite each teenager to find a partner, and give each pair one full page of a newspaper. Say: **There's an old saying that the Bible is as up-to-date as the daily newspaper. Of course, the Bible was written centuries ago, but many people think it still has relevance for us today. What do you think? Does God still love the world? Is there still evidence in the world of God's saving grace?**

bonus idea

Use this idea as a sermon on a youth Sunday in your worship service. People of all ages respond to the message.

I'd like each pair to look through its section of newspaper and find evidences of God's love for the world. You might find this evidence in a classified ad, a photograph, a feature story, an editorial, or a headline. Use your imagination and faith. In a moment, everyone will have an opportunity to tell the group what he or she discovered about God's love.

Give teenagers several minutes to complete the task. During this time, play soft background music or upbeat contemporary Christian selections which might stimulate thought or spark the imagination.

After each pair has found a newspaper article or advertisement it would like to talk about, begin your worship time by singing a few songs. You might include a simple song like "Jesus Loves Me." Invite someone to again read aloud the Bible verse projected on the wall.

Then tell the teenagers that they will be giving the sermon. Invite members of each pair to give a one- to two-minute talk about what they found in their newspaper section as evidence of God's love.

Following this sermon, have everyone read John 3:16 aloud in unison. Close with a song or prayer.

WIND CHIMES

COST: *$5-$15*
WORK LEVEL: *easy*
TIME INVOLVED: *instant*
MATERIALS: *assorted wind chimes*

Several years ago, an elderly woman presented our youth group with a set of wind chimes. It was a lovely piece of art that made high-pitched whistles whenever the wind blew across the myriad of tiny reeds. The only trouble was, we had no place to hang it outside, and there was no wind indoors. The chimes ended up inside after all, though, and we stared at them all winter long as they hung silently in one corner of the room.

Eventually, we came to love those chimes. The kids discovered all kinds of ways to make them emit their high-pitched whistles. They blew on them, fanned them, and whirled them. The chimes became a curiosity piece for several of the teenagers, who seemed charmed by their haunting sound.

Since then, I've discovered many different kinds of wind chimes. Some are made of metal or pottery and emit their sound as the rods or other pieces clink against each other. Some make no "sound" at all, but they're beautiful to behold—swirls and spirals of various hues dancing in the air. Other chimes make beautiful sounds when you tap them with a stick.

Wind chimes can be found at yard sales, in novelty shops, in discount stores, and in duty-free shops at airports. Many chimes are made overseas from various types of wood, pottery, or bone. Few cost more than $15.

You can use chimes to decorate light fixtures, highlight seasonal decor, or stimulate conversation. They really add a lively and unexpected element to a youth area.

worship idea

Sounds of Praise

THEMES: *joy, praise*
MATERIALS: *Bibles*

Bring in several sets of wind chimes, and use them as part of this simple act of praise. Give everyone in the group a Bible, have kids sit in a circle, and have kids begin to take turns reading aloud verses of Psalms 112, 113, and 114. As students are reading these psalms, encourage other group members to make melody with the chimes. Pass the chimes around the circle as each psalm is read, verse by verse.

Close your time of praise by reading aloud together Psalm 150.

NEON SIGN

COST: *$200-$1000+*
WORK LEVEL: *difficult*
TIME INVOLVED: *short-term*
MATERIALS: *a neon sign*

Something about this youth room was definitely different. The room was darkened, but lights were blazing, flashing, and pulsating. After a few moments, I realized what it was: This group had a neon sign! This was one of the most unique touches I've seen in any youth room.

When I asked the youth leader about the sign, she told me the members of the group had checked at several lighting stores and advertising firms. Eventually they had ended up buying a neon sign from a sign company. There they found a cool neon logo that seemed custom-made for their youth center.

Neon lighting instills a room with a sense of friendship and excitement. A rheostat can enable you to dim neon lights for worship times, vespers, or other occasions.

Getting a neon sign with a desirable logo will take a chunk out of your budget. After a few phone calls you should be able to locate a decent sign for $200-$500. You might also need to check on wiring in your youth area, and you may need to make provisions for special electrical needs. If installation is needed, plan to add an extra fifty percent to the cost. Many signs, though, will simply plug into a wall socket.

devotion

Salt of the Earth, Light to the World

THEMES: *discipleship, faithfulness, sharing faith*
MATERIALS: *Bibles, a Bible dictionary, postcards, postcard stamps, and pencils or pens*

Before the devotion, look through a Bible dictionary and mark entries that talk about salt and light.

Darken the room (but be sure it's not too dark for reading and writing), and turn on your neon sign. Give each person a Bible, and invite the teenagers to turn to Matthew 5:13-16. Read aloud the passage about being salt of the earth and light to the world and then ask:

● What do you think it means to be salt of the earth?

● What do you think it means to be light to the world?

Have several volunteers read the entries you've marked in the Bible dictionary and then ask:

● What can we learn from the Bible dictionary about what it means to be salt and light in the world?

Give each person a postcard and a pencil or pen. Say: **Being salt of the earth and light to the world aren't easy tasks, but we can fulfill them with God's**

bonus idea

Instead of having teenagers write post-cards to others, you could offer an appropriate story or reflection from your own life concerning a time when someone was salt or light to you. This could be in the form of a short story, a drama, or a monologue.

You might want to bring in salt and flashlights for the devotional. Sprinkle a few grains of salt into the teenagers' palms and allow them to taste it as they think about what salt is and does. Distribute small flashlights, and allow the teenagers to shine these in the darkened room.

help. One way we can spread light to others is by demonstrating or talking about our love for God. Use your postcard to write a letter to someone you know who might be feeling low, depressed, or in need of a kind, uplifting word. Take this opportunity to be salt and light to that person.

Once the teenagers have written their postcards, make sure they've filled out the addresses. If they don't know the addresses of the people they've written to, tell them you'll call them the next day to get the addresses. Collect the cards, attach postage, and send them out the next day.

Have kids read aloud Matthew 5:13-16 again, taking turns reading a verse at a time. As the group reads aloud, turn off the neon sign and bring up the lights.

SCULPTURE

COST: *$200 and up*
WORK LEVEL: *easy*
TIME INVOLVED: *instant*
MATERIALS: *a sculpture*

Not every youth area could make use of a fine piece of art, but I have seen some wonderful sculptures gracing the hallways, foyers, and entrances of youth centers. Most of this art is of the modern variety—angled pieces of wood, pottery, or metal with bright colors—abstract presentations that convey as much emotion as thought. I've also seen sculptures of famous personalities from history, the church, and the Bible. One or two youth rooms I've visited featured papier-maché busts of pastors or youth leaders.

Sculptures are expensive. You might rate a good deal with a local sculptor if you know one. But otherwise you should plan to spend well over $200 to get a piece of art worthy of a spot in your youth area. If you're industrious or you love art, you might want to check out a local art show. You might be surprised by a good deal.

Since a sculpture is often seen as a needless commodity in the church, you should expect some resistance from church members. Art is rarely appreciated by the majority of the faithful—unless, of course, you're talking about stained glass, oil paintings of the Second Coming, or black-velvet paintings of Jesus kneeling in the garden of Gethsemane. Before purchasing a sculpture, do your homework and prepare your explanation well.

object lesson

The Fine Art of Faith

THEMES: *the Bible, faith*
MATERIALS: *modeling clay, Bibles, toothpicks, buttons, and beads*

Begin this object lesson by saying: **Today we're going to make our own sculptures. There's only one stipulation: Your sculpture must reflect—abstractly or otherwise—a Bible story.** For example, you might choose to use the modeling clay, buttons, and beads to make miniature figures telling the story of the Prodigal Son (Luke 15:11-32). Or you might use a few toothpicks, clay, and buttons to fashion a sculpture about the Apostle Paul's shipwreck on the way to Rome (Acts 27:13-44).

bonus idea

Purchase a sculpture that you can use as an object lesson itself. Look for abstract qualities that will lend much in the way of interpretation and creativity of thought. Try to draw biblical or theological themes from the work of art.

Allow time for each teenager (or each team if you prefer) to complete a sculpture. Be prepared to offer a list of biblical stories that might lend themselves well to this activity (try Genesis 2:7-17; 1 Samuel 6:1-9; 2 Kings 6:1-7; or Luke 20:20-26). Afterward, give each teenager an opportunity to tell about his or her sculpture and to read the appropriate Bible story.

Have kids form a circle with all the sculptures in the center of the circle. Ask:

● **What did you learn while you were creating your clay sculpture?**

● **How does each of these clay sculptures remind you of God's mystery and power?**

● **What do the various Bible stories represented by these sculptures tell us about faith?**

Encourage each student to use his or her clay sculpture to retell the Bible story to someone in the coming week. Perhaps a teenager could use the sculpture to teach a child, to lead a children's message in church, or in a Sunday school class.

DISPLAY CAROUSEL

COST: *$100-$200*
WORK LEVEL: *easy*
TIME INVOLVED: *instant*
MATERIALS: *a display carousel of any type*

Here's another idea to get important information to your youth group—use a display carousel. There are two basic types: a revolving carousel with several sides which can be filled with posters, letters, and other items; and a flip carousel (usually used to display posters in retail stores) which can be filled with photographs, cork board, and fliers.

One advantage to the display carousel is that it can be moved anywhere in the youth room or from one nonpermanent space to another. It can be placed by the door so teenagers will see it as soon as they enter, or you can make it a focal point near the center of the room. You can also use a display carousel to post your event calendar (p. 24) or to highlight Christian-music posters (p. 21).

bonus idea

Allow students to use the display carousel to post favorite Bible verses, posters, or poems that have helped the teenagers grow in their faith.

Many office-supply stores sell display carousels for less than $200. You might also be able to find them at going-out-of-business sales in retail stores. Having a display carousel can save you some time and postage, and you can also give your teenagers an opportunity to post their own announcements, prayer concerns (p. 32), cards, and letters.

Year at a Glance

THEMES: *planning, preparation*
MATERIALS: *poster board, markers, tape, and a display carousel*

Here's another way to involve your group in an annual planning event. Before the meeting, label seven pieces of poster board with these headings: "learning," "retreats," "just-for-fun events," "discussion topics," "outreach," "mission," and "service." You might also include other headings appropriate to your program.

Spread out your labeled sheets of poster board on the floor, and give each person a marker. Have kids form teams of three to five. Say: **Today we're going to look ahead to a new year in the youth group. I'd like each group to begin with one poster, brainstorm things that fit in that heading, and write down as many ideas as you can. When I call time, each group will switch to another poster and repeat the process.**

If you have more teams than posters, you may want to either encourage kids to work together with other teams on the same poster or create more than one poster for each heading.

Every four to six minutes, call time and allow the groups to shift. Make sure each group has a chance to write down ideas on each poster.

When you have completed this phase of the process, tape the posters to the wall. Work with the teenagers, helping them discuss and narrow down the ideas in each category until you have a degree of consensus on a reasonable number of ideas. Work with the students to assign dates to the activities on the lists. Allow the teenagers to prepare a final draft of each poster, including the dates. Place the final posters on the display carousel.

This entire process should take a while, so plan to use your entire youth meeting as a planning session. Encourage the teenagers to pray about the upcoming events and to flip through the display carousel from time to time to keep abreast of youth group activities.

ideas: creative furnishings

Locations

LIMOUSINE

COST: *$30-$150*
WORK LEVEL: *easy*
TIME INVOLVED: *instant*
MATERIALS: *a rented limousine*

This idea is obviously one you wouldn't use on a regular basis, but it can make your meeting an unforgettable time of celebration. A small youth group in North Carolina used a limousine service for a youth meeting. They hired a limo to pick them up at the church, meander through the country-side, and return them to the church an hour later. During this time they engaged in Bible study, group planning, and prayer.

Perhaps you've considered using alternative meeting-sites for your group. Maybe you don't have enough space in your current facility, you don't have a youth center, or you have no permanent meeting-space anyway. Perhaps you simply want to conduct a creative meeting from time to time. Whatever the reason, meeting in a limousine can be fun and unique.

Limousines rent by the hour, and the prices vary in different parts of the country. You can expect to find a basic limousine (seating six to eight) for $30 to $75 an hour. A stretch limousine (seating eight to twenty-five) will rent for $5 to $15 an hour more. Also, some services expect you to tip the limousine driver. You should ask about this policy beforehand, or expect to add an extra fifteen to twenty percent to the total bill.

Now consider everything you can do in a limo. You can experience a topical lesson, a Bible study, a prayer time, or a learning moment. You can also create some challenging scavenger hunts (looking for license plates, signs, or roadside objects). And a limo makes an exciting place for a planning retreat. Often our creativity

126

is heightened when we move ourselves out of the familiar sur-
roundings of church or home. A new look and a fresh perspective
on the world around us can spark new ideas.

If you're thinking about hiring a limousine service, plan to
shop around. There should be several limousine services listed in
your Yellow Pages. Prices vary, as does the quality of the limousines themselves.

group builder

Limo Leadership

THEMES: *leadership, planning*

MATERIALS: *a Bible, pencils, index cards, masking tape, paper, and a calendar*

bonus idea

Shuffle your leadership
team every year so new
insights and ideas are
included.

Use your one- to two-hour limousine ride as a group planning-
session for a new year. Invite your leadership team to take part in
this special event. The time you spend in the limousine can be used wisely and well. Using this format,
you should be able to conduct a productive planning
session in less than two hours.

Begin your planning session by reading Matthew
7:24-27 aloud. Then ask:

● As you think about this Scripture, how do you think it applies
to our youth group?

● Where is our group weak? Where is it strong?

● How can we use these words of Jesus to build a better foundation for our group?

● As we think about preparing for another year in our youth
group, what should we consider most important in our planning?

Give each person a pencil and an index card, and say: **Take a
moment to write your responses on the index card.**

When kids have written their responses, collect the cards and read
them aloud. Make note of the most important considerations and then
tape the cards to the wall.

Give each person a piece of paper, and ask the teenagers to think
about three areas of group life: Learning, Laughter, and Love. Say: **Take
a few minutes to write down your ideas for upcoming events. Make
three columns on your paper—a column for ideas that can help us
learn, a column for ideas that can help us laugh and have fun together,**

and a column for ideas that can help us reach out to others in love.

Allow several minutes for this task. Then, using a clean sheet of paper, begin to compile all the ideas presented by the teenagers in each of these three areas. Spend at least thirty minutes discussing these suggestions. Then begin to narrow the ideas to a manageable number.

For example, you might operate on a fifty-two-week schedule. On a calendar, mark off the weeks you won't meet as a youth group. Then pencil in the special events that are annual traditions. This should leave you with a good idea of how many learning events, fun events, and outreach events you can schedule.

As you mark up the calendar, take note of those school days and vacation times that may offset your special activities. By planning ahead, you should be able to arrange a memorable year for the youth group.

If you have time remaining in the limousine, close your planning session by reviewing the calendar, praying, or, if you prefer, singing a wacky song.

When your limousine ride is over, spend a few minutes making a master calendar for the upcoming year. Post this master calendar on the wall, or plan to make copies for everyone in the youth group. You might want to use this master calendar to make a group directory of upcoming events, listing dates, times, and cost. This kind of advance planning allows kids to fit special events into their own busy schedules and to work with parents to cover extra costs.

GAZEBO

COST: *$700-$1000*
WORK LEVEL: *difficult*
TIME INVOLVED: *short-term*
MATERIALS: *lumber and hardware or a gazebo kit*

Years ago, when I was serving a rural church in North Carolina, our youth group was forced to meet for a while in a small gazebo outside the church. The church building was under construction, and there was no place else to go. But that gazebo was a blessing in disguise. It turned out to be one of the best possible meeting places for our group that summer.

A gifted carpenter could build a gazebo in a day, or you could purchase the gazebo in a kit with the pieces already assembled. All you would have to do would be to bolt the pieces together. These gazebo kits can be found at many lumberyards, home-improvement stores, hardware stores, and yard- and garden-shops. An average gazebo can seat a dozen people comfortably (some can seat two dozen), and most are constructed of treated wood.

Should you begin looking for a gazebo, expect the prices to vary widely. Some can be found for less than $700; others cost more than $2000, with an average around $1000. But as with so many other items, quality does vary from company to company. Make sure your kit is composed of treated lumber, is prestained, and comes with assembly instructions.

Obviously, gazebos are warm-weather meeting places. They make excellent small-group discussion areas (and for this reason I've seen many of them at church camps), but they can also be used as winter-storage areas. During the cold months, a gazebo can be covered with plastic.

Before you purchase your gazebo, make sure you have a firm, level place to erect it. The church board will no doubt have an opinion about having this feature on the church lawn (if that's where you want to put it). Point out that the gazebo can be used for many other purposes, including church picnics, children's classes, adult Bible studies, a place of fellowship, and decor.

ideas: locations

Christians Under Construction

THEMES: *cooperation, gifts, teamwork*
MATERIALS: *a gazebo kit and tools*

Once you have your gazebo kit, plan to use the youth group to construct it. This will make a fine work-project and will bring the group together. You'll also need a few adult helpers (particularly carpenters), plenty of hammers and nails, power tools, and any other items listed in your gazebo-kit instructions. Depending on the type of gazebo you purchase, you might also need stain or paint and brushes. Make this an exciting event for teenagers, parents, and other people from the church.

Plan to begin your work project with a prayer and a brief devotion about cooperation. Read 1 Corinthians 12:12-31 aloud. Then say: **One of the marks of being disciples of Jesus is that we work together. We all have different abilities and talents, but when we complement each other, we can do so much more together than we could ever do alone. I hope this project will serve to bring us together, teach us patience and kindness, remind us that we're the body of Christ, and give us a beautiful place to meet.**

bonus idea

After the work project is finished, take the time to ask these questions:

● **What did you learn from building this gazebo together?**
● **What made this project tough?**
● **How do you think this gazebo can be used for God's work in the future?**
Close with prayer inside the gazebo or standing around it.

Ask:

- What does it mean to be the body of Christ?
- What does this passage say about cooperation among the people of God?
- How can we work together to accomplish the will of God?

Following this discussion, lead the group in completing the work project, making sure each young person is involved in some way— either by working directly on the gazebo, by providing refreshments and drinks for the workers, or by helping with errands.

TENT

COST: *$80-$1000*
WORK LEVEL: *moderate*
TIME INVOLVED: *short-term*
MATERIALS: *a tent*

In a way, tents are an important part of our spiritual heritage. Abraham and Sarah lived in a tent (Genesis 12:8), the Israelites lived in tents in the wilderness (Exodus 33:8-10; Numbers 11:10), and they worshiped in a tent (Exodus 40). The Apostle Paul was a tentmaker by trade, as were Aquila and Priscilla (Acts 18:1-3). And many of the early Christian ascetics lived in tents. With all this history behind us, why shouldn't we all take to our tents from time to time?

Actually, setting up a youth meeting in a tent might prove to be an easy task. Many families camp out on a regular basis. Some take vacations in tents, and others just like to set tents up in backyards. So you may have a host of small tents readily available to you.

In the event that you'd like to plan a tent outing with your youth group and you need to purchase a tent or two, you can find a four-adult tent for less than $80 in most department stores and in major mail-order catalogs. Larger tents, which sleep six to eight people, can be purchased for less than $130. Depending on the size of your group, you can have a wonderful campout for a small investment. And once you have the tents, you can use them year after year.

If this type of tent camping doesn't appeal to you and you're looking for something on a larger scale, you might call a local tent-rental business. Most of these suppliers will erect a "circus style" tent or canopy to your specifications. These rental tents, though, will range in cost from $250 to $1000, and you'll only be able to use them once. Nevertheless, if you're planning a large outdoor youth rally, a concert, or a giant slumber party, this might be the way to go.

Once you've decided to get a tent, consider the possibilities for your group. In addition to campouts, you can use the tent for worship experiences, devotional times, and games. To provide a change of pace, you might also use the tent for a regular youth meeting. Teenagers enjoy new places, and a tent can provide a new setting for discussion and learning.

devotion

Fear Not!

THEMES: *the Bible, faith*
MATERIALS: *Bibles and flashlights*

Swat mosquitoes, roast marshmallows, and then gather around the campfire for this evening devotion.

Begin by inviting teenagers to tell a few scary stories or share personal accounts of fear. Once everyone is in a spooky mood, begin the devotion by asking this question:

● **What are your greatest fears in life?**

Listen carefully to teenagers' answers and then add a few of your own.

Divide the teenagers into three groups. Assign one of these Scripture passages to each group: Matthew 28:1-8; Luke 1:1-30; and Luke 5:1-10. Then ask each group to discuss these questions:

● **In your Bible story, what fears are mentioned?**
● **How were these fears overcome?**
● **Does your faith in God help reduce your fears? Why or why not?**
● **How has God helped you overcome your fears?**
● **What has God promised us concerning our fears?**

Close with a few uplifting campfire songs and a prayer.

ALTERNATIVE MEETING-PLACES

COST: *$0*
WORK LEVEL: *easy*
TIME INVOLVED: *instant*
MATERIALS: *none*

Perhaps you've been looking for that perfect retreat site for a weekend getaway for the youth group. If so, chances are you can locate a house, cottage, or cabin that would be just right for you.

Over the years I've found some unique houses in which to conduct youth meetings. I once used a river cottage for an overnight planning session. On another occasion a friend of mine loaned us his spacious basement—complete with a billiard table, a jukebox, a computer, and virtual reality toys—for a youth game-night. I've also conducted meetings in a teepee, a business office, a jail, a church camp, a retreat center, a beach cottage, a courtroom, and a funeral home.

As you begin to network within your congregation and among friends, no doubt you will find many alternative sites for youth meetings. Network by asking some of the key leaders in your congregation if they know any judges (who might let you use a courtroom or jail space), retirees (who might let you use a vacation cabin), or funeral home directors (who might let you use a funeral home). These alternative locations don't have to be far from your regular meeting site to be fun and productive. From time to time we all need a change of scenery. Locating an alternative location for a meeting can be one way of staving off boredom, sparking creativity, or attracting a few new teenagers.

crowdbreaker
Balloon Portraits

THEMES: *friendship*
MATERIALS: *balloons (light colors work best) and felt-tip pens*

Try this crowdbreaker at your next alternative meeting-site to help kids feel comfortable and energized in your new setting. This idea is also a wonderful way to introduce and welcome new teenagers to your group.

As kids arrive at the alternative site, give each person a balloon and have the teenagers blow them up and tie off the ends. Then say: **Every one of us is unique. None of us looks exactly like another person, and we should always celebrate that fact. Using the felt-tip pens, take a few minutes to draw your self-portrait on your balloon. Be creative, and be prepared, in a moment, to introduce yourself to the group using your balloon.**

After teenagers have completed their balloon self-portraits, allow teenagers to introduce themselves to the others, one at a time. You may also want to post the following instructions on the wall:

Give us the following information:

● your name
● your grade
● your school
● your hobbies
● your strangest habit
● your happiest moment

Seasonal Decor

CEILING MASKS

COST: *$0-$25*
WORK LEVEL: *easy*
TIME INVOLVED: *instant*
MATERIALS: *assorted masks and tape or tacks*

In a youth room in Denver, I saw a very creative ceiling-decorating idea for Halloween. Each teenager had secured a Halloween mask to a light fixture, bringing the room alive with a sea of funny, scary, and prominent faces. Not only did these serve as decor for the Halloween party, but the masks also provided inspiration for the evening lesson (see the object-lesson idea on the following page).

Ceiling masks are a seasonal idea that can add color and variety to your youth center. If you have teenagers bring or make their own masks, they cost you nothing and the kids will gain much enjoyment from contributing.

bonus idea

Instead of masks, decorate the ceiling with T-shirts, caps, hats, or festive items such as piñatas.

135

Unmasking Our Fears

THEMES: *death, faith, fear*
MATERIALS: *a collection of masks*

Next Halloween, try using a few masks as an object lesson. Allow each teenager to bring, make, or choose a mask. Find a funny mask, a sad mask, and a frightening mask among their selections.

Begin the object lesson by asking:

● **When you look at each of these masks, what feelings do you experience?**

● **Why did you bring** (or make or choose) **your particular mask?**

When teenagers have responded, relate the history of Halloween (All Hallows Eve). You can find a history of Halloween in an encyclopedia or in a book about holidays. (Halloween originated as a Celtic festival to honor the god of the dead. In the ninth century, the Christian church established All Hallows on November 1 in honor of the saints and All Souls' Day on November 2 to honor the souls of the dead, particularly those who had died in the preceding year.)

Ask:

● **Why do you think people throughout history have feared death?**

● **Do you think people today fear death? Why or why not?**

● **How do people in our society respond to the reality of death?**

Following discussion, invite a volunteer to read aloud 1 Corinthians 15:12-14, 35-44.

Say: **These masks are reminders that each of us will die someday. But God tells us that death isn't the end. Jesus came to be our Savior. He died for our sins, rose from the grave, and overcame death's power. The Bible tells us that those who receive by faith Jesus' sacrifice on their behalf will also overcome death. He will live in us, and by faith we will live in him. And even though we still have a fear of death, we know that Jesus has removed the sting of death. Every time we put on a Halloween mask, let's remember God's power to overcome death. The masks can remind us that all of our days—happy days, sad**

bonus idea

Read 1 Corinthians 15:54-57. Then have a time of prayer for the group or, if you prefer, read a list of those teenagers or other church members who have died in the past year, giving thanks for their faithful witness and lives.

days, and fearful days—belong to God. And God will see us through every trial of this world and into the world to come.

PLOW

COST: *$0-$75*
WORK LEVEL: *easy*
TIME INVOLVED: *instant*
MATERIALS: *a hand plow*

Periodically you may want to decorate your youth area with an object that will provoke questions from teenagers: "What's this doing in here?" An old-fashioned hand plow will certainly get the job done. A plow may look out of place to most teenagers, but it can make an excellent object lesson.

bonus idea

If you're using your hand plow in the spring or summer and you have a garden near the church, allow the teenagers to plant some flowers or vegetable plants. Later the group can harvest the vegetables and sell them as a fund-raiser or give them away.

You may be able to find an old-fashioned one-furrow hand plow in an antique shop or at a farm and garden store. Or if you're adventuresome, check out a few country auctions. You can often find a good deal on used farm equipment. Prices on old hand plows will vary widely, but you should be able to find a decent plow for less than $75.

A plow can make good decor in the springtime. Good Scripture references include Amos 9:11-15; Micah 4:1-5; and Luke 9:57-62. Good topics to explore with the plow include war and peace, planting and reaping, and faithfulness to the tasks of God.

devotion

Swords Into Plowshares

THEMES: *peace, violence, war*
MATERIALS: *Bibles, index cards, pencils, and newspapers*

Use the plow to lead this active-learning devotion about peace.

Begin by distributing the newspapers. Ask each teenager to find a news story about violence, injustice, or war in our world. Then, in groups of three or four, have teenagers read their news stories to each other.

Give each person an index card and a pencil. With the teenagers still in their small groups, say: **I'd like you to think about the true stories of violence and war you have just read. Using your index card, write down a few of your ideas about how we can have a more peaceful world. For example, how can we work to overcome violence and war?**

After groups have completed their index cards, allow the groups to discuss their ideas. Have one person from each group share these ideas with the other groups.

Give each person a Bible. Have the group members turn to Micah 4:1-5. Read the passage together and then ask:

● **What was the vision of the prophet Micah?**

● **What do you think he meant when he said people would make their swords into plowshares?**

● **Why do you think violence has always been a part of our world?**

● **How can we apply Micah's vision of peace to our world today?**

● **What can our youth group do to make the world a less violent place?**

After this discussion, distribute the newspapers again. This time ask teenagers to search for stories that describe how people have settled their differences peacefully or cooperatively. In small groups, ask teenagers to share these stories.

Close the devotion with a time of confession. Encourage kids to admit that they haven't always lived peacefully and that they need God's help to overcome anger and violence. Offer words of pardon and forgiveness and then have everyone join hands and say a prayer together.

ROCKS

COST: *$0*
WORK LEVEL: *medium*
TIME INVOLVED: *instant*
MATERIALS: *rocks or small boulders*

Your youth area will make a strong impression once you bring in a couple of boulders. Rocks make excellent discussion starters, and they can be painted, polished, or decorated. I had never seen rocks in a youth area until I visited a church in Colorado that used the theme "Jesus Is the Rock." This youth group had painted scenes from the Bible on the boulders, making the room come alive with color and story.

No matter where you live, you should have very little trouble finding a few rocks. Check out a nearby stream or river—there are usually plenty of stones at the water's edge—or a forest preserve or public park. Or if you live in a farming community, you may be able to find some rocks near a field. In the event that you can't find a rock, you can always go to a lawn and garden center and buy a decorative rock, but these are no different than the ones you can find on your own.

Should you want to decorate your rock, try using some interior latex paint. On a clean surface, this should hold up quite well. You might also use ribbons or cloth to add color to a rock display.

When you go rock hunting, be sure to bring along a pair of work gloves, a small shovel or pick, and a partner. You won't want to lift heavy rocks by yourself. And please...watch your toes!

---

devotion

Rock 'n' Roll Bible Hunt

THEMES: *the Bible, faithfulness, patience*
MATERIALS: *Bible concordances, Bibles, paper, and pencils or pens*

Since there are numerous references in the Bible to rocks, use your rocks as an opportunity to help teenagers learn how to use a Bible concordance.

Have teenagers form a circle and then divide

bonus idea

If you don't want to use the Bible concordances, you may want to assign a specific Scripture passage to each group. You might try some of →

these Bible passages: Numbers 20:1-12; Matthew 4:1-11; Matthew 7:24-27; Luke 6:46-49; John 8:1-11; and John 11:17-44. These would make excellent skit material, and most teenagers would be able to formulate a creative presentation.

bonus idea

Close your devotion with a reading from Psalm 18:1-3 or with a time of singing and praise.

the students into teams of four to six. Each team should have its own concordance and a Bible. Say: I'd like each team to look in the concordance and find the word "rock" or "stone." When you've found the word, look underneath it to find some Bible references that contain that word. Look up several of the Scripture passages and read them aloud to your team. Then, with your team, choose the passage you like best.

When each team has completed this part of the devotion, add these instructions: Now I'd like each team to create a skit or another type of presentation that will illustrate the Scripture passage it has chosen.

When each team has completed preparations for its skit or other presentation, designate a stage area and give each team an opportunity to act out, sing, or dramatize the Scripture lesson dealing with "rock" or "stone." Encourage teams to use the rocks in your youth area as props.

WATER DISPLAY

COST: *$25-$50*
WORK LEVEL: *easy*
TIME INVOLVED: *instant*
MATERIALS: *a water display such as a fountain, a wishing well, or a water wheel*

There are many types of water displays you can use in your youth area. Bridal shops, home and garden centers, and hardware stores carry a variety of fountains, wishing wells, and water wheels you can purchase or rent for a day. Most of these can be rented for less than $50.

A water display makes an excellent centerpiece for a large youth rally or a great complement to a lesson on baptism. Other groups in the church could also use the water display.

At a gathering of pastors, I noticed that a water display had been set up to illustrate the theme "Wellsprings of Healing." Be creative. Consider biblical themes of life, energy, hope, creation, wholeness, and healing. Most likely you'll be able to think of numerous ways to use your water display.

Living Water

THEMES: *faith, hope*
MATERIALS: *Bibles*

Have kids form two groups. Assign one team to read Matthew 14:22-36 and the other group to read John 4:1-26. When each group has read its Scripture passage, ask:

● How did water play a role in the Bible story?
● How did Jesus use water to teach about faith?

Have the entire group gather around the water display. Allow the teenagers to dip their hands into the water and then ask:

● What are some ways we use water in the church?
● What other Bible stories come to mind as you touch the water in this water display?
● What can this water illustrate for us about faith and hope?

bonus idea

Other great water stories from the Bible include Genesis 1:1-2, 6-10; Exodus 15:22-27; Exodus 17:1-7; Matthew 10:42; and John 2:1-11. If your group is very large, have kids form several teams and assign additional Bible stories.

ideas: seasonal decor

AQUARIUM

COST: *$80-$100*
WORK LEVEL: *moderate*
TIME INVOLVED: *long-term*
MATERIALS: *an aquarium, aquarium supplies, and fish*

Ever walked into a youth room and noticed something fishy? Ever wished you could talk your teenagers into becoming fishers of people? Look for an aquarium—it can

bonus idea

After you purchase your aquarium, buy one fish for each member of the youth group. Allow each person to name his or her fish. Trying to identify and keep track of these fish each week is hilarious.

make a great object lesson. You can find an aquarium in any general retail store for less than $100 (usually as a kit). Tanks can sometimes be found for as little as $10.

But don't forget the fish. Add a few bucks if you want to buy a couple of quickly multiplying fish like guppies. Just make sure you get a male and a female! Not all fish are inexpensive—some exotic species can cost $20 apiece or more. Be sure to ask the salesperson which types of fish mix well with other varieties.

Once you get your aquarium, you're certain to find a few teenagers gravitating toward the fish tank. You might even pick up a youth group mascot in the deal (maybe a turtle or a piranha). An aquarium can add a new dimension to the youth area and bring a little life to an otherwise drab room. (Just don't forget to feed the fish!)

object lesson

Miracles Galore

THEMES: *faith, miracles*

MATERIALS: *Bibles, an aquarium treasure-chest, a waterproof marker, and an aquarium net*

Before the meeting, write one of these Bible references on the inside of the treasure chest with a waterproof marker: Matthew 14:13-21; Luke 5:1-7; or John 21:1-13. Then dump the chest into the aquarium. Have teenagers gather around the aquarium, and ask:

● **How would you describe a miracle to someone else?**

After kids respond, allow a volunteer to use the net to retrieve the treasure chest from the aquarium. In your own words, retell the story of the miracle described in the Scripture passage referred to inside the treasure chest. Then ask:

● **What was the problem in this story?**

● **What did Jesus do?**

● **How would you describe the miracle in this story?**

● **What miracles might be happening around us today?**

● **How have you seen God work in similar ways in your life?**

PUMPKINS, WHEAT, AND CORN

COST: *$0-$25*
WORK LEVEL: *easy*
TIME INVOLVED: *short-term*
MATERIALS: *pumpkins, wheat, and corn*

During the fall months, try decorating the youth area with pumpkins, bundles of wheat stalks, and ears of corn. These make colorful centerpieces for tables or can add a warm flair to a cold room. You can find pumpkins and corn in grocery stores, and wheat stalks are available in craft stores. With a little effort, though, you should be able to obtain them free.

Pumpkins, wheat, and corn are seasonal decor, but they can also be used for fund-raisers, games, and discussion starters. For example, you can collect many of these items, make them into beautiful centerpieces, and sell them. Or you can have pumpkin-cleaning contests or relay games.

And if you're looking for a fun fall outing, try a visit to a pumpkin patch and a hayride.

bonus idea

If you have time, try baking a few pumpkin seeds. They're a delicious snack food. Clean the seeds, and place them on a cookie sheet with a little oil. Sprinkle them lightly with salt. Bake at 350 degrees until they're golden brown. Eat 'em like popcorn!

---

crowdbreaker

Pumpkin Symbols

THEMES: *the church, faith*
MATERIALS: *pumpkins, pumpkin-carving kits, markers, and newspapers*

Give each teenager a pumpkin and a carving kit, or have kids form teams and give a pumpkin and a kit to each team. Have kids empty their pumpkins, putting the pulp and seeds on newspaper. Say: **I'd like you to carve a Christian symbol into your pumpkin. Try to be creative. And be prepared to explain your symbol to the rest of the group when finished.**

When everyone is finished carving, allow time for teenagers to show off their pumpkins.

bonus idea

If you think your teenagers might need help thinking of some Christian symbols, have a book of symbols on hand or suggest symbols such as the cross, a dove, praying hands, a butterfly, a fish, a hand, or a watchful eye.

FLOWERS

COST: *$5-$25*

WORK LEVEL: *easy*

TIME INVOLVED: *short-term*

MATERIALS: *assorted garden flowers, flowerpots, and potting soil*

When the world begins to blossom with spring fever, why not let your youth area bloom along with it? Invite teenagers to bring in various wild flowers, garden flowers, or starter sets. Pot them, arrange them, and distribute them throughout the room. You might find that you have a few future gardeners in the group.

Also, try some hanging baskets in the corners. These are great for petunias (if you have natural light in your room). Just don't forget to water them.

A room full of bright flowers can make a huge difference to a youth group still emerging from the winter doldrums.

fund-raiser

Flowerpots

THEMES: *none*

MATERIALS: *flowers, plastic pots or hanging baskets, and potting soil*

bonus idea

If you prefer not to do this as a fund-raiser but would like to make a difference to someone else, use the activity as a service project instead. Take your potted flowers to nursing homes, hospitals, children's homes, or group homes for the developmentally disabled. These small gifts can brighten someone else's room for an entire summer.

Visit a local flower shop or greenhouse, and purchase a number of seedling flowers or young sets that are ready to plant. Organize your group to follow potting instructions to make a number of pots and hanging baskets full of flowers. Advertise these for sale in your church newsletter. You should be able to make a nice profit, since many people regularly purchase new flowers each spring. This is one way you can meet a need and have a successful fund-raiser at the same time.

In-Room Fund-Raisers

RECYCLING BINS

COST: *$0-$30*
WORK LEVEL: *easy*
TIME INVOLVED: *long-term*
MATERIALS: *plastic storage bins or plastic garbage cans*

More and more youth groups are using in-room fund-raisers as a source of income. In-room fund-raisers save time and energy. Many are low-maintenance (requiring no cleanup or setup). And they can also be long-term sources of revenue, which means that a group might need fewer fund-raisers in the course of a year.

Consider placing recycling bins in your youth center. These can be storage units of any type or variety. You can purchase plastic garbage cans (which are not too terribly unattractive and could be placed in a corner) for around $10 each. And often waste-disposal companies will provide containers for a small deposit or for free. These recycling bins can be used for aluminum cans, newspapers, tin cans, glass, plastic, or cardboard. The revenue produced from recycling can add up quickly, especially since more and more industries are demanding recycled products.

With a little advertising, you can include the entire church in your efforts. Many church members would be glad to bring cans, newspapers, or other used products to help the teenagers.

bonus idea

One youth group had a bin for paperback books. These books were taken to a used bookstore and traded in for cash (ten cents to a quarter each). People from the church and community used the service, and the group had a consistent income each month.

Aluminum-Can Crunch

THEMES: *cooperation, teamwork*

MATERIALS: *two hand-operated can crunchers (about $10 each) and a collection of aluminum cans*

O nce you get a bin full of aluminum cans, begin a meeting with this fun game of skill and cooperation. Before this game, make sure all the cans are completely empty.

Have kids form two teams, give each team a can cruncher, and then divide the aluminum cans evenly among the two teams. Each team must form a human chain, passing the cans along like a bucket brigade. The first team to successfully crunch all its cans wins.

Teams can also make up funny fight-songs, cadences, or slogans to help spur them on.

(sidebar, rotated) **ideas: in-room fund-raisers**

PENNY DROP

COST: *$0-$20*

WORK LEVEL: *easy*

TIME INVOLVED: *long-term*

MATERIALS: *a sturdy, covered container (such as a garbage can)*

A s the old adage says, "A penny saved is a penny earned." But what can you buy these days with a penny? Not much. But you can buy a lot if you have a million of them. Then you have a cool $10,000!

How long would it take for your group to collect a million pennies? a year? two years? five? Start now and think long-term. Have an annual churchwide penny drive. You'll be amazed at how many people will add to the collection. You can store the pennies in a garbage can and empty it from time to time, making bank deposits, or you can wait until you've reached your goal to cash the pennies in.

bonus idea

For years a good friend of mine conducted this unique coin fund-raiser for mission work. Each Sunday (for four consecutive Sundays) he would invite the →

146

congregation to place pennies, nickels, dimes, and quarters in the offering plates. The results were amazing. It was always his best fund-raiser of the year.

One group went so far as to construct a huge bin, capable of holding a million pennies, in the center of the youth room. People could roll their pennies one by one down a long track that emptied into the bin. Believe me, a million pennies is quite an impressive sight. And heavy!

When you go to cash this load, you'd better have a few pickup trucks handy. Oh...and don't forget to tell the bank you're coming in. They'll be thrilled.

crowdbreaker
Penny Search

THEMES: *cooperation, teamwork*
MATERIALS: *a pile of pennies*

After you get a large pile of pennies, have a bit of fun with your stash. Have kids form teams, parcel out the pennies, and invite the teams to go in search of pennies from twenty-five consecutive years or tell students the first team to find a penny from each year from 1950 through the current year is the winning team. Give extra points for any "wheat" pennies or other "wheat" coins (nickels, dimes, or quarters) that are discovered.

NEWSPAPER TRAILER

COST: *$0*
WORK LEVEL: *easy*
TIME INVOLVED: *long-term*
MATERIALS: *a trailer large enough to hold several tons of newspaper*

One Indiana youth group was able to organize a citywide newspaper-recycling service. They asked the church board for permission to park a semitrailer (owned by a local recycling center) in one corner of the church parking lot. People dropped their newspaper at this drop-off site, and the youth group was able to ship out several tons of paper four times a year. It was a hefty moneymaker, and the recycling center (which received a share of the profits) was grateful for the additional revenue.

Perhaps your group couldn't fill a semitrailer, but a smaller trailer filled with newspaper could certainly net you several hundred dollars each year. Look into locating a pull-behind trailer or a dumpster that isn't being used. Get the word out to the community and the church that you have a newspaper-recycling center. You might soon be shipping out a few tons of material every year to a recycler.

devotion

Used News

THEMES: *discouragement, drugs and alcohol, faith*
MATERIALS: *newspapers and Bibles*

Distribute a stack of newspapers among students. Invite teenagers to find stories about people who have taken wrong turns in life, who have become addicted to drugs or alcohol, or who seem to be mixed up with the wrong crowd.

Once everyone has found a story or two, invite the teenagers to share what they have found. Use these questions to help teenagers focus on the deeper issues:

bonus idea

If you have extra time after your devotion, use this time to cut out comic strips for your "Wall of 'Toons" (p. 35).

● Why do you think this person made these mistakes?

● In what ways does this person need help?

● How might this person's problems be addressed from a spiritual perspective?

Give each person a Bible, and ask everyone to read 1 John 5:1-15. Have volunteers paraphrase the passage in their own words. Then ask:

● According to this passage, who is Jesus?

● What does this passage say about the power of faith?

● What does this passage tell us about overcoming life's temptations and obstacles?

● Do you think it's possible to make a change of direction in life? Why or why not?

● What are some ways we can live in God's strength?

Refer students back to the newspaper stories they discussed earlier. Invite teenagers to think about the many ways in which people live without faith. Then ask:

● How could these stories have turned out differently if the people involved had faith in Jesus?

● In what ways could the church help the people in these situations?

● In what areas of your life do you need to be challenged and need to change so you can live more wholeheartedly for Jesus?

Close the devotion by reading a positive story of faith and hope from the newspaper.

SPIRIT TOWELS

COST: *$25-$75*
WORK LEVEL: *moderate*
TIME INVOLVED: *short-term*
MATERIALS: *solid-colored cotton hand-towels, fabric paints, and a silk-screen stencil*

Ever wish you could pass along the spirit of your youth group to the rest of the church? Try making spirit towels—they're easy.

First come up with a group logo, Scripture verse, or design. Go to a local craft shop or custom T-shirt store, and have them make a silk-screen stencil of the idea (for about $25). Then purchase a supply of hand towels, set up an assembly line, and start screening.

Simply lay the stencil over each towel and then dab various colors of paint through the pattern and onto the towel. Using this method, you should be able to turn out several dozen spirit towels in no time.

These spirit towels make wonderful Christmas gifts, and many church members would love to catch some of the youthful vigor your group represents. Hang

bonus idea

If you're looking for some neat artwork for your spirit towels, check out Group Publishing's clip-art books and disks.

the towels in your youth room as decor. And, if you feel adventuresome, take orders for full sets of bath towels.

worship idea

Cleanin' Up

THEME: *forgiveness, love, servanthood, sin*
MATERIALS: *a basin of water, a Bible, and spirit towels*

If you've ever wanted to try a foot-washing ceremony with your teenagers, the spirit towels might provide a perfect opportunity to stretch their faith and love. Have kids gather around a basin of water. Set a somber mood by dimming the lights, playing soft music in the background, or strumming a guitar.

Read slowly from John 13:1-17. Then say: **This story tells us much about the Christian life. Jesus responded to our sin and evil by demonstrating how to serve. He gave his disciples—including you and me—an opportunity to show the world how much we care for each other. When Jesus washed the disciples' feet, he was showing that we need to be willing to do even the simplest acts of kindness, humbling ourselves before God and before each other. Jesus became like a servant. He humbled himself, demonstrating that even small things make a difference in the kingdom of God, especially acts of service to others. When we decide to follow Jesus, we take upon ourselves this same type of service to others that Jesus demonstrated.**

Pause for a time of silent confession and then offer words of pardon (or have a volunteer read from Psalm 51:1-17).

Invite the teenagers to take turns washing one another's feet and drying them with spirit towels. Close your worship experience by singing songs of joy or listening to upbeat Christian music.

Creative Closets

CLOSET OF COSTUMES

COST: *$0-$50*
WORK LEVEL: *easy*
TIME INVOLVED: *short-term*
MATERIALS: *closet rods, storage boxes, and shelving*

Most youth rooms have closets in desperate need of transformation. What does yours look like? Is it a disorganized mess of basketballs, Frisbees, Christmas ornaments, and dogeared Bibles? Does it reek with the aroma of old cheese? Is there something small and furry lying in the corner?

Don't despair. Transforming a closet can be exciting, especially if you have something to put inside it. And that's where the costumes come in.

bonus idea

If you don't have a youth room with a closet, try using large wardrobe boxes or a "portable closet"—a frame with plastic or fabric covering (available at discount stores).

Once you've cleaned your closet, secured a few rods, added a few shelves, and thrown in some mothballs, you can get down to some serious closet creativity. Invite teenagers to bring in old Halloween costumes, Mom's and Pop's ancient threads from decades long gone, and stuff from the attic. Sort the costumes by size, type, or era, and place some in labeled boxes and hang others in sections on the rods.

Knowing you have the stuff on hand, you'll think of dozens of ways to utilize the costuming. Use the clothing for skits, dramatizations of Scripture, creative dialogues, or role playing. Have a Halloween party in April. Organize a costume ball. Throw a masquerade party.

dramatization

Returning Thanks

THEMES: *grace, thankfulness*
MATERIALS: *costumes and a Bible*

This dramatization of Luke 17:11-19 (the healing of ten lepers) is a fine way to stress thankfulness in the Christian life. This dramatization should involve everyone in your youth group, as you can have as many as twenty-three people in costume (ten lepers, Jesus, and twelve disciples). If you have more than twenty-three students, allow the rest of your group members to play a crowd that watches and comments on the event. Allow the teenagers to be creative with their costuming and portrayal of the action. You might be able to perform this dramatization more than once in order to discover different nuances of meaning implicit in the text.

bonus idea

If your group is particularly gifted with acting ability, talk to your pastor about dramatizing other Scripture readings for Sunday morning worship.

Allow kids a few moments to dress in costumes and then, as a narrator reads the biblical text, cue the teenagers to act out the scenes. After the dramatization, ask these questions:

● What did you learn from this story?
● Why do you think only one person returned to give thanks to Jesus?
● With whom did you most identify in the story?
● What would be a modern-day equivalent to the skin disease leprosy?
● What does this story tell us about how we should respond to people who are hurting?

153

CLOSET OF MAGIC

COST: *$50-$100*
WORK LEVEL: *difficult*
TIME INVOLVED: *long-term*
MATERIALS: *assorted magic tricks*

When I was a teenager, a magician visited our church. She performed amazing card tricks, broke through chains, and made oranges disappear into thin air. She also managed to convince me that there was a Christian message in each trick—a feat greater than all the others combined.

Over the years I've wondered how many other Christian magicians are out there. They seem to be rare, but this idea just might help change that.

Take interested teenagers to a magic shop and let them make their own selections. This will help them develop responsibility and determination.

If you'd like to encourage a new generation of magicians, buy a few magic tricks, place them in your youth-room closet, and invite teenagers to perfect one or two of them. Hold a magic-trick night in which interested teenagers get to show off their skills. Challenge teenagers to use the magic tricks to communicate Christian principles or lessons.

You can find a large selection of magic tricks in novelty stores or magic shops, and you should be able to buy a potpourri of tricks for less than $100.

service project
Mission Magic

THEMES: *love, service*
MATERIALS: *magic tricks*

If you have teenagers in your group who have become skilled in performing magic tricks, why not take your show on the road? Many children's homes, homeless shelters, hospitals, and youth centers would enjoy this form of entertainment. You can weave in a Christian message, hand out balloons, and make a real show of love.

Helping teenagers organize and perfect this type of ministry may be challenging, but the rewards can be great. Imagine an entire youth group working its magic on others.

CLOSET OF CLOWNS

COST: *$50-$75*
WORK LEVEL: *difficult*
TIME INVOLVED: *long-term*
MATERIALS: *shelving, closet rods, clown costumes, face paints, and wigs*

Many youth groups have clown ministries in place, but there is still growing interest in this creative form of message and drama. If your group has been considering this type of ministry, you'll certainly want to establish a place to store all the costumes, paints, and wigs.

With a bit of money and effort, you should be able to renovate an existing closet and purchase basic clowning supplies for less than $50. Clowning supplies are usually available in novelty shops or through clowning catalogs.

Once your closet is complete, encourage teenagers to pick up clowning costumes and makeup at the church. This setup could become a real boost for your teenagers who are looking for ways to be in ministry to others.

dramatization
The Trickster

THEMES: *dishonesty, Jacob and Esau, trickery*
MATERIALS: *face paint, clown costumes, paper, pens or pencils, and a Bible*

bonus idea

Find a clowning ministry in your area, and invite that group to your youth meeting. Allow your teenagers to see how this ministry can be an effective way of communicating the gospel. This may spark interest in beginning a clowning ministry in your church.

Try a dramatization of Genesis 27:1-35 (Jacob tricks Isaac and steals Esau's blessing) in clown costumes. Appoint a narrator to read the Bible story as clowns portray the action. You'll need people to play Isaac, Rebekah, Jacob, and Esau. If you want to add more characters and more laughs, allow other students to play the parts of inanimate objects and animals (such as the two goats, the pot of stew, and the tent).

While the clowns are dramatizing the Bible story, invite other teenagers to jot down impressions or observations.

Following the drama, discuss these questions:

● What observations and impressions did you have of Jacob? of Isaac? of Rebekah?

● What does this story tell us about dishonesty and trickery?

● How did the clowns help you understand this Bible story?

● What does this story tell us about family relationships?

After the discussion, encourage kids to spend a few minutes thinking about other ways they can use the clowning supplies in ministry. Think about service projects and church events where you could offer a clowning ministry.

CLOSET OF MUSIC

COST: *$50-$100*
WORK LEVEL: *easy*
TIME INVOLVED: *long-term*
MATERIALS: *shelving and assorted musical instruments*

Any youth group with musical talent should have a closet of instruments. I'm not talking about trumpets, trombones, and saxophones but instead about an assortment of smaller instruments that anyone can use: kazoos, bongo drums, wood blocks, maracas, and tambourines. Imagine the fun you could have with such a band.

Check out the music stores in your area. You should be able to pick up an assortment of these instruments for less than $100. Place them in labeled boxes in the closet so you'll have them on hand whenever your group feels the urge to make music.

You can use the instruments in your closet of music to accompany skits, sing-alongs, object lessons, or Christmas caroling. And since these instruments are small enough to fit in a box, you can take them anywhere—even to retreats, campouts, and lock-ins.

bonus idea

When you replace your old musical instruments with new ones, give your old instruments to the children of the church or donate them to a mission.

Make a Joyful Noise

THEMES: *adoration, music, praise*

MATERIALS: *musical instruments, Bibles, index cards, and pencils or pens*

Have kids gather around the boxes of assorted instruments. Invite each teenager to pick an instrument that he or she enjoys playing.

Have kids spend a few moments reading aloud Psalm 148:1-13. Encourage them to read with expression and enthusiasm. Give each person an index card and a pencil or pen. Say: **People of faith have given praise to God in different ways throughout time and across cultures. Most of the time, we praise God for all that God has done for us and for all that God gives us. Take a few moments to jot down a few things you're thankful for and then we'll take turns reading our blessings as we give thanks to God.**

When each person has had an opportunity to list his or her items on his or her index card, have students take turns reading their lists aloud. After one person reads his or her list of blessings, let all the students make a joyful noise on their instruments. Proceed around the circle in this manner until everyone has had a chance to name his or her blessings one by one.

Close the time of praise by reading Psalm 150. Whenever teenagers hear the words "praise the Lord," "praise God," or "praise him," have them play their instruments.

CLOSET OF T-SHIRTS

COST: *$0-$75*

WORK LEVEL: *easy*

TIME INVOLVED: *long-term*

MATERIALS: *closet rods and shelving*

For decades, teenagers have loved T-shirts. Clothing stores abound with them, and the T-shirt industry is a multibillion-dollar-a-year business. Most youth groups have gotten into the act by making their own T-shirts for mission trips, fun outings, and group identity.

I've noticed that most youth groups have lots of extra T-shirts on hand. These leftovers are usually given away or placed in rummage sales, but they can be used in other ways.

Consider transforming your closet into a clothing center. Hang all your old T-shirts on a rack and use them for skits, outings, and retreats. These older T-shirts could also be sold to raise funds. The more variety you have, the more likely teenagers will enjoy a closet of T-shirts.

If you have the money, buy several T-shirts in various styles, make your own logos, personalize a few shirts, and see what happens. In a short time you may find that you've found a marketing niche. Next thing you know, you'll be trying to think of a name for your clothing store.

discussion starter

Memories

THEMES: *the church, fellowship, memories*
MATERIALS: *assorted T-shirts from past mission trips, group outings, and other events*

Spread your T-shirt collection on the floor. Allow the teenagers to look at the collection for a few minutes. Then say: **Each of these T-shirts is associated with a special time in the youth group. These times were special and meaningful. Some of you may remember these times, or you might know people who were involved in the youth group then.**

Have kids form a circle and then ask:

● What memories come to mind as you look at these T-shirts?

● Why are memories important to us?

● What do you want to remember about your youth group?

● Can you think of a special time we've shared together?

● What was your funniest experience in the youth group?

● Can you think of a special youth event when you felt especially close to God?

bonus idea

If you don't have a T-shirt collection built up, invite teenagers to bring in some of their favorites from home (as long as they're appropriate). Use the discussion starter to talk about what these T-shirts mean to them and the memories associated with them.

Other Fun Ideas

SUGGESTION BOX

COST: *$0*
WORK LEVEL: *easy*
TIME INVOLVED: *instant*
MATERIALS: *a homemade box or another container labeled "Suggestions," slips of paper, and pencils or pens*

Here's a simple idea: the good old suggestion box. Think it seems out of date? I tried this idea once and was amazed to find that many teenagers and parents were offering anonymous tips—mostly aimed at topics they would like to discuss or activities and work projects they would like to try. The reason? Perhaps many were too shy to offer suggestions to a "professional." Or maybe they were afraid to express their opinions in public. The suggestion box provided a way out.

Whenever I speak with teenagers about fear, I find that one of their greatest apprehensions is speaking in public. This might go a long way in explaining why restaurants and businesses offer their customers an opportunity to express their feelings on small cards. Most folks have an aversion to offering verbal suggestions—even good ones.

Make your suggestion box out of an oatmeal container or a cardboard box. Cover it with construction paper, label it, and you're ready to go. Place the box near the door of the youth room, and leave a few slips of paper and pencils or pens nearby.

Take a peek every month or so, and you'll be impressed with the suggestions your teenagers have offered.

Love Letters

THEMES: *communication, love*

MATERIALS: *a Bible, several sheets of stationery, pencils or pens, a suggestion box, and a chalkboard and chalk or newsprint and a marker*

Have a volunteer read from Ephesians 5:19-20 or Colossians 3:15-17. Then say: **The Scriptures tell us to lift each other up, to give thanks to God for all things, and to offer words of praise. We often do that for God but fail to do it for each other.**

Give each teenager a piece of stationery and a pencil or pen. Say: **I'd like each of you to write a letter of appreciation to the rest of the group. Express how you feel about the people in the group. And at the bottom of your letter, give your suggestions for new ways we can better love and appreciate each other.**

While the teenagers are working on this, write a letter of appreciation to the entire youth group. Make this a heartfelt effort to express how you feel about your teenagers. Offer any suggestions you have about how the youth group members might better accept and love one another.

After everyone has completed a letter, collect the letters and place them in the suggestion box. Invite teenagers to take turns drawing out letters and reading them aloud. Make notes of suggestions on a chalkboard or a piece of newsprint. Finally, read your letter to the group and encourage everyone to follow the suggestions on your list.

Allow the group to spend a few moments in silent prayer for each other and then join hands and sing a favorite group song.

bonus idea

As an alternative to having kids write general letters of affirmation and place them in the suggestion box, you could have students draw names out of a hat. Each teenager would write an anonymous letter of appreciation to one other person in the group. Collect the letters, hold onto them for one month, and then mail them to the respective teenagers. Everyone in your group will be surprised by the letter, and your teenagers will learn how much they are cared for and appreciated by others.

ideas: other fun ideas

PROFESSIONAL BANNER

COST: *$200-$400*
WORK LEVEL: *easy*
TIME INVOLVED: *instant*
MATERIALS: *a professionally made banner and supplies to hang the banner*

Here's a great outreach or advertising idea. If your youth group has a special event coming up or wants to be more intentional about inviting others, you might consider purchasing a professional banner. Most of these banners are made to order and are composed of weatherproof plastic or canvas. You can hang your banner on the outside of your event site. On a busy street, thousands of people might see the banner on an average day.

ideas: other fun ideas

bonus idea

When you're pricing your banner, see if the advertising firm will print on the front and on the back of your banner. Some places won't charge as much for a second message. Thinking ahead may save you time and money in the long run.

One church, located next to a high school, has used banners over the years to invite many new students to its events. Decide on the best way for your group to use this type of banner. For major annual events, banners can be used many times. Simply paint over the old dates and times and stencil in the new ones. Banners can be quite effective in drawing large groups of teenagers to an event. And they're a great way of reaching out to the community through a visual display.

Price a banner at a local advertising business. A professional banner measuring four-by-six feet usually can be purchased for less than $200. Longer banners will, of course, cost more.

publicity project
Spreading the Word

THEMES: *outreach, publicity*
MATERIALS: *a stack of special-event fliers and adults to provide transportation (optional)*

Displaying a professional banner for a special event can definitely stir up excitement among the members of your youth group. For example, if your group wants to advertise an upcoming Christian rock concert or evangelistic event, you could use the banner to help rally your own teenagers to spread the word.

First, decide on the best location to hang the banner. Then plan the following outdoor activity. Have kids form teams of two. Give each pair a handful of fliers describing your special event.

Say: **Jesus once sent pairs of disciples into the villages to proclaim the message of God's kingdom. Today we have an opportunity to invite friends and strangers to be a part of our upcoming event. Because we want to spread the message of God's love, we're inviting others to join us to learn more about God. Take your fliers to other churches, hang them in public buildings, or give them to other teenagers. Speak to people you meet, and spread the word.**

Depending on the nature and size of your community, you might send the teenagers out on foot or have adult drivers standing by to assist with transportation. Set a time limit for the activity.

When all the teams have returned, have the entire group help hang the banner in a prominent place where people driving by will notice it. Then discuss these questions:

● What did you learn from this experience?
● Who did you meet? What did you say?
● Do you think this was an effective way to get our message out to people in our community?

EXERCISE BIKE

COST: *$300-$500*
WORK LEVEL: *easy*
TIME INVOLVED: *instant*
MATERIALS: *an exercise bike*

I've noticed that more and more churches are offering physical fitness and aerobics programs in their facilities. One reason for this is that families are looking for places where they can not only worship together but also enjoy recreation and have fun. A few larger youth centers I know have also included weight rooms and running tracks.

Having an exercise bike in the youth room might be a good starting point if you're looking toward this type of ministry. Teenagers (and adults, for that matter) can sign up to ride the bike. Young people who are involved in athletic activities may also want to work out in the youth room before or after meetings.

Exercise equipment ranges widely in price, and you often get what you pay for. If you're looking at buying a piece of equipment, I recommend that you never go below $300 when looking for a stationary bike. The best ones cost around $500. Top-of-the-line equipment can be found in retail stores, although the larger chains tend to carry more fragile models. I recommend a sporting goods store—one that specializes in heavier athletic equipment such as treadmills, stair machines, rowing machines, and stationary bikes. You'll probably find something to meet your budget.

bonus idea

If you want to get really funky with your bike-a-thon, try one or more of the following ideas: enlist adults to ride the bike instead of teenagers, place the bike in the back of a truck and "ride around town" as a promotional gimmick, use a "tag team" approach—allowing a group of teenagers to switch when they get tired, or ride the bike on Sunday mornings in the fellowship center to draw attention to your project.

fund-raiser

Bike-a-Thon

THEMES: *missions, teamwork*
MATERIALS: *an exercise bike and a sign-up sheet*

Wouldn't it be nice to have a bike-a-thon without ever leaving the youth room? You can if you have a stationary bike. All you'll need are a few young people who are willing to keep the pedals turning for a worthy mission project, a sign-up sheet, and a bunch of people who are willing to make pledges based on the number of hours, miles, or minutes the teenagers ride.

You could even use the fund-raiser to pay for the bike itself.

ideas: other fun ideas

MAIL SLOTS

COST: *$40-$50*
WORK LEVEL: *easy*
TIME INVOLVED: *instant*
MATERIALS: *cardboard or plastic mail-slot kits, labels, and markers*

Go to an office-supply store and find a cardboard or plastic mail-slot kit. These kits are easy to assemble and will usually provide fifty slots that can serve as mailboxes. Label each slot with a name, attach this arrangement to the wall or place it on a counter top, and you have an instant post office in the youth room.

Many groups are using this type of setup in lieu of mailing out newsletters, postcards, and letters. This saves time and postage, and teenagers learn to take responsibility for their attendance and participation. A few youth leaders I know place their group newsletters in these mail slots. After a couple of weeks, they then mail the newsletters that haven't been picked up by the teenagers. This takes extra time, but it does save on postage.

If you have a large youth group or you simply want to encourage your teenagers to stay active in the group, mail slots could be just the thing you need.

bonus idea

Four times a year, place a personal, handwritten letter in the mail slot of each teenager in your group. This is one way to let your young people know you care about them.

ideas: other fun ideas

---

skit

A Little Mouse Told Me...

THEMES: *outreach*
MATERIALS: *mail slots, youth group newsletters or fliers, a mousetrap, and a pencil*

Choose two actors to play the parts in the skit on page 166. You'll need a mail clerk and a postal worker. Before the skit, set a mousetrap and place it inside one of the mail slots. Be sure the actors in the skit know which slot the trap is in.

After the skit, use these questions for discussion:

- How could we do a better job of reaching out to others?
- Can you think of people who might need the support of our group?

- What events could we organize that would help us reach more teenagers?
- Who could you invite to a youth event next week?

STROBE LIGHT

COST: *$30-$50*
WORK LEVEL: *easy*
TIME INVOLVED: *instant*
MATERIALS: *a strobe light*

For your next lock-in, evening gathering, or overnight event, get a strobe light. It's an easy way to add some flair to any selection of music, and a strobe light can liven up any game.

You can find strobe lights in most music stores and in pawn shops. Most range from $25-$50.

This is one of those items you may not use often, but it's nice to have a strobe light around, particularly for special events.

group builder

Back to the '70s

THEMES: *popular culture, trends*
MATERIALS: *a strobe light, a selection of disco music, a record player or an eight-track tape player and records or eight-track tapes, '70s-style clothing, and party snacks*

bonus idea

Find selections of Christian rock-music from the '70s. Play these to show the teenagers how all styles of music have changed through the years.

Help your group plan a '70s party, complete with disco music, bell-bottom pants, and your strobe light. Enlist some teenagers to bring selections of their parents' '70s music. Other teenagers can bring clothing, vintage '70s items, and snacks.

You can also play popular '70s games such as Twister, The Game of Life, and Pit. Don't forget to have fun with hair styles. And if you happen to get the chance to make videotapes of popular '70s TV shows,

A Little Mouse Told Me...

Script:

*(Inside the local post office, the **Mail Clerk** is sorting the morning mail, stuffing youth group newsletters or fliers into the mail slots. Another **Postal Worker** enters and immediately seems concerned.)*

Postal Worker: Hey, don't stick your hand in there!

Mail Clerk: *(Startled, jumps away from the slots.)* What? What's the matter?

Postal Worker: Don't you know we've got a mouse on the loose?

Mail Clerk: A mouse? Is that all?

Postal Worker: Take a look in there. *(Pointing to the slot with a mousetrap inside.)*

Mail Clerk: *(Looking inside the mail slot.)* Hey, someone put a mousetrap in that mail slot.

Postal Worker: I did. Last night.

Mail Clerk: But I could have stuck my hand in there. I could have broken a finger.

Postal Worker: Don't worry. *(Uses a pencil to snap the mousetrap.)* Can't hurt you now.

Mail Clerk: Thanks.

Postal Worker: Hey, what are you sorting?

Mail Clerk: Looks like something from a church youth group.

Postal Worker: *(Picks up a flier and reads a few of the announcements.)*

Mail Clerk: That sounds like a happening bunch of teenagers.

Postal Worker: Maybe I ought to send my kid over there. He could use some help.

Mail Clerk: Oh, problems on the home front?

Postal Worker: Nothing big. He just needs a little guidance. You know what I mean?

Mail Clerk: *(Hands the **Postal Worker** a flier.)* Hey, look at this…that mouse has struck again. It chewed the mailing label off this newsletter. Why don't you give it to your son? Tell him a little mouse sent you.

Postal Worker: Maybe I'll do that. Thanks. And hey…watch out for that mousetrap!

show the teenagers a few clips from "The Sonny & Cher Comedy Hour," "The Tonight Show" (Johnny who?), "Hawaii Five-O," or "Mannix."

MANNEQUIN

COST: *$0-$100*
WORK LEVEL: *easy*
TIME INVOLVED: *short-term*
MATERIALS: *store mannequins and costumes*

OK, so maybe mannequins aren't anatomically correct, but they can add some wonderful flair to your youth room. Put one of your youth group T-shirts on a mannequin, and the shirts will be a guaranteed sell.

Furthermore, it's a lot of fun to change the poses and costumes of the mannequins—just be careful not to make them look too kinky!

One group has a mannequin as a mascot. They've given him a name, they take him on outings, and they keep him dressed in the most current seasonal fashion. The mannequin even went on a Halloween retreat without his head!

You might be able to obtain a mannequin from a department store. Some larger merchandisers get new mannequins in from time to time and may be willing to part with the older ones. A store manager in your congregation may be able to work something out for you. And many retailers would be willing to part with a mannequin as a tax write-off if you tell them it's for a church youth group. If not, you should be able to find a mannequin for around $100.

One helpful word of warning, though: Once you bring the mannequin into the church, refrain from placing it in a dimly lit hallway. Mannequins have been known to give unsuspecting custodians heart attacks.

Mannequin Mix-Up

THEMES: *none*

MATERIALS: *a mannequin and clothing for the mannequin*

This crowdbreaker will help your teenagers be observant and get to know each other better. Begin by giving each teenager an opportunity to say his or her name and describe a favorite outfit that he or she likes to wear.

bonus idea

Be sure to provide a closet, a restroom, or another place for teenagers to change clothes. You could also use your closet of costumes (p. 152), closet of clowns (p. 155), or closet of T-shirts (p. 157) for this event.

Next, invite the teenagers to work together to dress the mannequin, using the clothing you have provided. Have kids form two teams. One team will leave the room for a moment while the other team adds or removes an article of clothing from the mannequin while switching it with an article of clothing or jewelry taken from one of the team members.

Have the first team then re-enter the room and identify the individual (by name) who has switched clothing with the dummy. Naturally, less conspicuous switches will be more difficult to spot. This crowdbreaker can be hysterical and can lead to some unique clothing combinations as the two groups take turns dressing and undressing the dummy.

ideas: other fun ideas

Indexes

programming-ideas index

theme index

Group Publishing, Inc.
Attention: Books & Curriculum
P.O. Box 481
Loveland, CO 80539
Fax: (970) 669-1994

Evaluation for *Meeting-Space Ideas for Youth Ministry*

Please help Group Publishing, Inc., continue to provide innovative and useful resources for ministry. Please take a moment to fill out this evaluation and mail or fax it to us. Thanks!

● ● ●

1. As a whole, this book has been (circle one)

not very helpful   very helpful

1   2   3   4   5   6   7   8   9   10

2. The best things about this book:

3. Ways this book could be improved:

4. Things I will change because of this book:

5. Other books I'd like to see Group publish in the future:

6. Would you be interested in field-testing future Group products and giving us your feedback? If so, please fill in the information below:

Name _____

Street Address _____

City _____ State _____ Zip _____

Phone Number _____ Date _____

Bible Study Series

Give Your Teenagers a Solid Faith Foundation That Lasts a Lifetime!

Here are the *essentials* of the Christian life—core values teenagers *must* believe to make good decisions now...and build an *unshakable* lifelong faith. Developed by youth workers like you...field-tested with *real* youth groups in *real* churches...here's the meat your kids *must* have to grow spiritually—presented in a fun, involving way!

Each 4-session **Core Belief Bible Study Series** book lets you easily...

- Lead deep, compelling, *relevant* discussions your kids won't want to miss...
- Involve teenagers in exploring life-changing truths...
- Help kids create healthy relationships with each other—and you!
- **Plus you'll make an *eternal difference* in the lives of your kids** as you give them a solid faith foundation that stands firm on God's Word.

Here are the Core Belief Bible Study Series titles already available...

Senior High Studies

Why **Being a Christian** Matters	0-7644-0883-6	Why **Spiritual Growth** Matters	0-7644-0884-4
Why **Creation** Matters	0-7644-0880-1	Why **Suffering** Matters	0-7644-0879-8
Why **Forgiveness** Matters	0-7644-0887-9	Why **the Bible** Matters	0-7644-0882-8
Why **God** Matters	0-7644-0874-7	Why **the Church** Matters	0-7644-0890-9
Why **God's Justice** Matters	0-7644-0886-0	Why **the Holy Spirit** Matters	0-7644-0876-3
Why **Jesus Christ** Matters	0-7644-0875-5	Why **the Last Days** Matter	0-7644-0888-7
Why **Love** Matters	0-7644-0889-5	Why **the Spiritual Realm** Matters	0-7644-0881-X
Why **Personal Character** Matters	0-7644-0885-2		

Junior High/Middle School Studies

The Truth About **Being a Christian**	0-7644-0859-3	The Truth About **Sin and Forgiveness**	0-7644-0863-1
The Truth About **Creation**	0-7644-0856-9	The Truth About **Spiritual Growth**	0-7644-0860-7
The Truth About **Developing Character**	0-7644-0861-5	The Truth About **Suffering**	0-7644-0855-0
		The Truth About **the Bible**	0-7644-0858-5
The Truth About **God**	0-7644-0850-X	The Truth About **the Church**	0-7644-0866-6
The Truth About **God's Justice**	0-7644-0862-3	The Truth About **the Holy Spirit**	0-7644-0852-6
The Truth About **Jesus Christ**	0-7644-0851-8	The Truth About **the Last Days**	0-7644-0864-X
The Truth About **Love**	0-7644-0865-8	The Truth About **the Spiritual Realm**	0-7644-0857-7

Order today from your local Christian bookstore, or write:
Group Publishing, P.O. Box 485, Loveland, CO 80539.

BIBLE MYSTERY EVENTS
For Youth Ministry

It's a party...a Bible adventure...and a dress-up event— all rolled into one!

Here's a brand-new way to get teenagers (and adults) involved in Bible learning! They'll act out roles as they play fun games, and discover new insights into important Bible stories! Each game comes with complete instructions to design an event that lasts three hours...or three days...it's up to you!

Included: event invitations, character descriptions, decorating tips, clues, costuming ideas, menus, advertising clip art, Bible-application ideas, and a step-by-step planning guide.

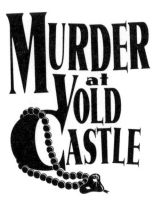

Robert & Linda Klimek

Visitors to this historic fortress discover their host, Baron von Schnell, has been killed...and every guest is a suspect! As your kids act out their roles, they'll experience the same intrigues and conflicts lived out by Saul and David—and prepare for an exciting Bible study.

ISBN 1-55945-694-9

THE CASE OF THE MISSING PROFESSOR

Robert & Linda Klimek

Not much happens in Wallar Hollar... except that the professor has disappeared! Somebody knows more than he or she is saying—but who? This down-home experience raises the same fear... confusion...joy...and surprise experienced by men and women who knew Jesus.

ISBN 1-55945-776-7

More Practical Resources for Your Youth Ministry

PointMaker™ Devotions for Youth Ministry

Here's active learning at its best—with 45 PointMakers™ that will help your teenagers discover, understand, and apply biblical principles. PointMakers work on their own for brief meetings on specific topics or slide easily into any youth curriculum to make a lasting impression. They're devotions with an attitude—getting your kids up and involved! **Included:** handy Scripture and topical indexes that make it quick and easy to select the perfect PointMaker for any lesson you want to teach!

ISBN 0-7644-2003-8

Quick Help!

Here are the practical solutions you've looked for to your most perplexing youth ministry problems—from ministry pros! You'll learn how to recruit and hang on to excellent volunteers...work with even unreasonable parents...balance professional and personal lives...get through to youth in ways that matter...and discover outreach ideas that *work*. BONUS: exhaustive table of contents organizes ideas by topics, so ideas are always at your fingertips!

ISBN 0-7644-2018-6

Youth Worker's Idea Depot™

Here are Group's 1,001 greatest ideas for youth ministry—on one convenient CD-ROM! Practical, proven ideas gathered from front-line ministry professionals make this a *gold mine* of ministry solutions! Save time! You can search these ideas instantly—by Scripture...topic...key words...or by personal notes you've entered into your database. And you can add your new ideas at any time! Save money! You'll get a complete library of ideas—plus a trial subscription to Group Magazine, where you'll discover dozens of new ideas in every issue!

Categories of ideas on your **Idea Depot** disk include: learning games, creative readings, adventures, object lessons, skits, retreats and overnighters, devotions, projects, affirmation activities, creative prayers, music ideas, creative Bible studies, and parties!

ISBN 0-7644-2034-8

Worship Ideas for Youth Ministry

Get your teenagers excited about worship—*and* about God! Each worship idea is based on a passage from the Gospels. Ideas include traditional forms of worship and exciting new ideas—perfect for starting youth meetings, developing a biblical theme, enjoying a special youth worship and prayer meeting...or helping youth lead an entire congregation in worship. If you're a youth worker, event leader, Christian club or camp director, or Christian school teacher, you'll use this collection of relevant, easy-prep worship experiences again and again!

ISBN 0-7644-2002-X

Order today from your local Christian bookstore, or write:
Group Publishing, P.O. Box 485, Loveland, CO 80539.